SURPRISES
BY THE RIVER

Also by Jon L. Berquist
Ancient Wine, New Wineskins:
The Lord's Supper in Old Testament Perspective
Reclaiming Her Story:
The Witness of Women in the Old Testament

SURPRISES
BY THE RIVER
The Prophecy of Ezekiel

Jon L. Berquist

Chalice Press
St. Louis, Missouri

Cover design: Samuel H. Dominguez
Photo: Vista III design
Art Director: Michael Dominguez

10 9 8 7 6 5 4 3 2 1

Library of Congress Cataloging–in–Publication Data

Berquist, Jon L.
　　Surprises by the river : the prophecy of Ezekiel / Jon L. Berquist
　　Includes bibliographical references.
　　ISBN 0-8272-3432-5
　　1. Bible. O.T. Ezekiel—Criticism, interpretation, etc.
　I. Title
　BS1545.2.B46 1993　　　　224'.4'06　　　　　　　93-23434

For Richard and Mary Beth,
with gratitude for beginnings
and the excitement of surprises

Acknowledgments

This book owes its origins to David Polk, the editor of Chalice Press, who challenged me to spend time with this recalcitrant prophet. As usual, David's proddings have improved the work. His visions may not be quite as grandiose as Ezekiel's, but they have been of immense service to the church nonetheless.

Thanks are also due to the churches who listened to parts of this work in progress: First Christian Church (Disciples of Christ), Caney, Kansas; Harvard Avenue Christian Church (Disciples of Christ), Tulsa, Oklahoma; Fellowship Lutheran Church, Tulsa, Oklahoma; and Jenks United Methodist Church, Jenks, Oklahoma. Also, portions were presented in 1991 to the Oklahoma Synod School of the Presbyterian Church (USA) in Oklahoma City and in 1993 to the Red River Preaching Workshop in Lake Murray, Oklahoma. A special thanks to

Laura Rey Spicer, whose careful reading of the first draft helped me to avoid several mistakes and encouraged me to continue with the project.

On a more personal level, my thanks go to those who have surprised me—whether by a river or in some more mundane part of life. My two years with Ezekiel have been full of surprises, both painful and pleasant. As I have experienced echoes of Ezekiel's loss and uprootedness, there have also been surprises of hope for new beginnings, and I find myself, like the book of Ezekiel, ending with plans for a new day of God's people. My thanks to those who have surprised me with support and with the rich promise of starting over.

Among those who constantly surprise and shape me are my parents. Richard and Mary Beth Berquist not only gave me my beginning, they brought me to faith and have brought me back to deeper faith over and over again. Through all of my life's surprises, they have stood with me and loved me, and I offer them my deepest thanks.

Contents

1

Down by the Riverside

Often, when we think about people in the Bible, prophets come quickly to our minds. That's a good thing, because the Bible has plenty of prophets. The Old Testament contains three long books about prophets (Isaiah, Jeremiah, and Ezekiel) and twelve shorter prophetic books (Hosea through Malachi), plus several prophets who appear in other stories (Elijah, Elisha, Nathan, Huldah, and many others). In the New Testament, many people thought that John the Baptist and Jesus were prophets, and Paul writes frequently about the proper use of prophecy in the early church. In fact, prophets are one of the few categories of persons present in both the Old and New Testament. Priests, kings, and elders are important in the Old Testament, and the New Testament focuses on apostles and disciples, but prophets are prominent in both.

1

But what *is* a prophet? We sometimes think of wild-eyed lunatics who wander through the desert eating locusts and sending God's wrath upon unsuspecting people, or we think of ponderous preachers who hold forth from their street-corner pulpits. Maybe we think of pious individuals whose lives of prayer and sanctity serve as wonderful examples for our own faith, or of mystics who predict the future and announce its mysteries to other people, or of persons who lose control of their own bodies in ecstatic fits, uttering strange sounds like unknown languages.

None of these descriptions fits all the prophets. Their variety makes any definition almost impossible. It seems that there is no one idea of what a prophet is, even in the Bible. Indeed, about all that can be said about prophets is that they bring a message of God to the people. But even that causes problems, because prophets are not the only ones who bring God's message. Old Testament priests taught about God to each generation, and New Testament apostles preached God's words to vast crowds. Sharing God's message is not unique to the prophets, but prophets focus on communicating God's words in fresh ways that often prove surprising.

There are many situations in life and many different parts of God's message that apply best to those situations. Thus, it makes sense that there are so many different ways to be a prophet; the mode of communication matches the message that the audience needs to hear. In this way, the audience shapes the prophet. The unique situation of the moment and the specific needs of the individual audience require certain types of prophecy in order to communicate God's message in the best way possible. Because of this, we can say that prophets are not born that way; they are made.[1] The situation shapes the form that the prophecy will take. If this is right, then our study of the prophet Ezekiel must begin with an investigation of his life. What were the issues in his day? Who was his audience?

---

[1] However, note that Jeremiah claims that he received a call to be a prophet before he was born (1:5).

Where did they live? What did they need to hear from God? When we know the answers to these questions, we will have gone a long way toward understanding this ancient prophet.[2]

Conflict and Conquest

Many ancient Israelites considered the days of the monarchy to be the nation's crowning glory. Certainly, King David (1000–962 B.C.E.)[3] and King Solomon (962–922 B.C.E.) brought wealth and prosperity to their little kingdom, and Israel achieved a fair amount of international recognition. It was never a world power in its day, but at least its people could hold their heads high, enjoying the prestige and advantage of being a strong nation. Though life had been good (at least for some) in the days of those early kings, those days were long past. Right after Solomon's reign, the kingdom split in two: to the north was Israel and to the south was Judah. Israel was the larger, stronger nation, but Judah contained Jerusalem, the traditional seat of the religion and the former capital city. The two nations never rejoined. When the history of the monarchy (1–2 Kings) remembered the long procession of kings, most of those kings were evil rulers who corrupted their nation's politics and religion. Though the monarchy produced the days of national glory, it also resulted in centuries of suffering for God's people in Israel.

---

[2] Several books offer thorough discussions of ancient Israel's prophets. A general introduction appears in James L. Ward, *Thus Says the Lord: The Message of the Prophets* (Nashville: Abingdon, 1991). For an extensive historical presentation, see Joseph Blenkinsopp, *A History of Prophecy in Israel from the Settlement in the Land to the Hellenistic Period* (Philadelphia: Westminster Press, 1983). An insightful theological discussion can be found in Walter Brueggemann, *The Prophetic Imagination* (Philadelphia: Fortress Press, 1978).

[3] The terms *B.C.E.* and *C.E.* are used for dates, standing for Before the Common Era and Common Era, respectively. These measures of dates are used by Jewish and Christian scholars who interpret the Bible in an interfaith context, and they refer to the same years as the more familiar measures B.C. (Before Christ) and A.D. (Anno Domini, or Year of the Lord).

Almost three hundred years after Solomon, the southern
kingdom of Judah had a good, strong king named Josiah
(641–610 B.C.E.). For the first time in years, the priests of
Yahweh supported the king as God's righteous leader.[4] Josiah
was an effective politician and military commander, too, and
Judah seemed on the verge of returning to its ancient glory.
Surely, Josiah was God's chosen one to bring the people into a
new era of faith and prosperity. But Josiah was suddenly killed
on the battlefield in a fight with Egypt at a place called Megiddo.
Egypt placed a puppet government on the Jerusalem throne
and nearly made Judah into one of its own colonies. After
Josiah, the nation never recovered from its shock. The next few
years saw several ineffectual kings in quick succession, and
once again things seemed grim.

Judah was alone in a hostile world. Almost a century
before, the huge empire of Assyria had destroyed the nation of
Israel, Judah's neighbor to the north. Now there was nothing
left of Judah's sister nation. Assyria had tried to conquer
Jerusalem, too, but had fled from the battlefield to attend to an
urgent crisis at home. A new power was emerging in distant
Mesopotamia, called Babylonia. Soon, Babylonia conquered
Assyria itself and became the world's dominant power.
Babylonia now threatened Judah and other nations nearby,
such as Egypt. Judah was trapped between a hostile Egypt on
one side and an expanding, imperialistic Babylonia on the
other.

Through delicate arrangements of appeasement, Judah was
able to survive another generation, but in 597 B.C.E., the

---

[4] "Yahweh" is the most probable ancient pronunciation of the name of
God in the Old Testament. Most modern English translations follow
Jewish tradition and refrain from spelling (or pronouncing) this name out
of respect for God. Instead, these translations (such as KJV, RSV, NRSV,
and NIV) render the name *Yahweh* as "the LORD," in small capital letters to
show the difference between God's name and the title "lord" (the Hebrew
word *'adon*, which can apply to God or to human lords). This book uses the
word *Yahweh* to restore to Christian tradition a sense of the particularity of
God and also the sense that these are ancient texts.

Babylonian armies conquered Jerusalem and took many of its inhabitants into exile, including Ezekiel. The Jerusalem leaders strove to maintain their independence, and they tried alliances with Egypt in order to gain power against Babylonia. This plan failed, and in 586 B.C.E., it all came to its end. The Babylonian armies defeated Judah and leveled Jerusalem.[5] Many of the prominent leaders in Judah were executed immediately. But Babylonia was not interested in killing all the people. Instead, it wanted to make Judah into a productive but thoroughly powerless colony. Once they had killed the most dangerous persons, they told most of the population to stay in the land. They should continue to farm and to produce as they always had, but their taxes would be paid to Babylonia now, and not to a king in Jerusalem.

Babylonia stole the wealth from Jerusalem. The army took all of the gold and expensive items they could find, even if those things were the temple's sacred items. It made no difference at all to the Babylonians what the wealth's source was, as long as they could carry it with them back to Babylonia. This decimated the economy of Judah, leaving it a poor and struggling province, but that was not a very great change, since Judah had almost always been a poor and struggling nation. But the Babylonian government required the seizure of another kind of wealth, as well. It captured people who had all sorts of practical skills and deported them to Babylonia. The royal family and the lower-level administrative personnel of the Judean monarchy possessed skills in managing governmental affairs that could prove valuable to the Babylonians, and the priests were also highly educated persons who controlled much of the society's knowledge and tradition. The Babylonians selected a group of royalty, politicians, scribes, priests, and others, and took them captive. The army marched these exiles out of Jerusalem and across the many miles to Babylonia, where they set up cities to house them.

---

[5] See 2 Kings 24—25 (and also Jeremiah 52) for the story of Babylonia's conquest of Jerusalem.

Not all of the Jews went into exile. When the armies came to Judah, there were several hundred thousand people living in the small kingdom, and maybe as many as a million. But only around 50,000 of these Judeans were taken into exile. Probably the Babylonian army slaughtered tens of thousands of others, but still 90 percent of the Judean population stayed where they were, with relatively little change in their daily life of farming and tending their flocks. The 5 or 10 percent who were Judah's elite, the best and the brightest from Jerusalem's royal court and from its temple, became Babylonian exiles in 597 and 586 B.C.E., and they remained there (with their descendants) for at least two generations.

Life in Babylonian Exile

For us today, *exile* is an awful word. We often relate it to another distressing word, *refugee*. In our embattled world, when nations change governments, the angry new leaders often cast out countless thousands of people. Because of their ethnic group or their social standing or their political opinions, these people lose everything that they ever owned and they leave their homeland, by foot, car, or boat. They go wherever they can find a place to stay. Refugees rarely ask for much; they know that they are the rejects of their own homeland's government, and they live as outcasts of the world.[6] In squalid refugee camps, they live with no hope of improving themselves unless they can take control of their government and turn the tables on the oppressors who sent them away.

The elite Jews who left their homeland under threat of force were not refugees of this sort, but they still suffered a great psychological loss. They had believed for all their lives that Jerusalem was God's favored city, and that no harm could

---

[6] Perhaps more terrifying are the political prisoners or others under attack who are not allowed to leave their homelands. In those cases as well the world wonders what to do, as it has debated over issues such as Palestine, Kuwait, Somalia, and Bosnia in recent years, not to mention the number of cases that never reach the popular media in the United States.

possibly come to those who lived on Yahweh's holy mountain. They had lived in the shadow of the great temple, which Solomon had built nearly four hundred years before. They had been their nation's strongest, most influential people, the ones who had given orders and had taken the best of all the nation's goods. They had been rulers in their own land, and now they were little more than slaves of the Babylonian Empire.

But the Jewish exiles were not poor. Certainly, they were slaves who could not control their own lives, especially in terms of politics and economics, but the Babylonians did not mistreat them. Some of the exiles performed government service, and they lived within the palace in the middle of the capital city, Babylon, the greatest city that the world had yet known. Others settled on rich, fertile farms near the Tigris or the Euphrates rivers, where they could have some local autonomy. They needed to work all day on their farms, since they could never again order others to do their work for them, but at least they had good farmland. These exiles lived much better than modern refugees; they had all the necessities of life. If the exiles complained, it was because of how much they had lost, not just because of how little they had.[7]

Royalty

Babylonia exiled Jerusalem's royal family, who were descendants of David. The last king of David's line to sit on the throne in Jerusalem had been a puppet named Jehoiachin. Once he was in Babylonia, the imperial officials imprisoned him, but eventually he was freed. Jehoiachin then became a favorite of the emperor, and he lived in the palace with other exiled kings from all the known world.

Jerusalem's governmental officials were trained professionals, just like the administrators of other nations. Babylonia

---

[7] For other biblical literature written during and about the exile, see Ralph W. Klein, *Israel in Exile: A Theological Interpretation* (Overtures to Biblical Theology; Philadelphia: Fortress Press, 1979); and Walter Brueggemann, *Hopeful Imagination: Prophetic Voices in Exile* (Philadelphia: Fortress Press, 1986).

took many of them and put them to work in administering the Babylonian Empire. During this time, the Empire was in an expansion phase. Each year they conquered additional territories around the world. With each expansion, the difficulty of administration increased, and the Empire needed more governmental officials faster than they could train them, so they took persons trained to govern other nations and made them Babylonian officials. Of course, there would have been very close supervision, and loyalty to the Empire would be both expected and enforced. Perhaps Jerusalem's highest-ranking leaders became middle-managers in the Babylonian Empire, or even the ancient equivalent of paper-pushers, but they did work in the imperial bureaucracy in jobs that used their training. For this work, they were rewarded with a relatively high standard of living and with the ability to live in moderate freedom within the world's most active, exciting city—Babylon.

Elders

The Babylonian army brought many rural leaders into exile, as well. It was not enough to remove only the national leadership; local authorities were also dangerous, and so they too marched into exile. As far as we know, only the politically experienced Jews who received governmental positions lived in the city of Babylon itself. All others, including Jews who had lived outside Jerusalem, were settled on the farms and in small cities. Quite possibly, almost all of these Jews settled several small communities grouped into one general area. There is extensive evidence of Jewish communities in and near the Babylonian city of Nippur.[8] Nippur is on the Euphrates River, a short distance south of the city of Babylon. In this area, the exiled and transplanted Jews farmed the fertile land near the river and also became involved in commerce and other activities. The river provided a major trade route throughout the area, and so Nippur saw a great deal of commerce go through

---

[8] I. Tzvi Abusch, "Nippur," in *Harper's Bible Dictionary*, ed. Paul J. Achtemeier (San Francisco: Harper & Row, 1985), pp. 708–709.

it. This created work and opportunities, and over the years more and more Jews became involved in the life of the area.

Around the farms and in the cities, the Jews kept a separate ethnic identity, at least for the first generation or two. The exiles duplicated as much of their former social structure as possible. That meant that the local elders from the old country remained extremely important in the new land of Babylonia. Groups of elders met together frequently and made the decisions of the community in exile. These persons who were accustomed to prestige in their former lives were able to maintain that privilege, perhaps because they were able to exercise the quality of leadership necessary to keep the community together. Nearly one hundred fifty years earlier, the Assyrian army had conquered the northern kingdom of Israel and had scattered its inhabitants throughout the empire; the Israelites lost their identity and were never brought together again. The elders of Judah knew that cultural survival in Babylonia would be most difficult, and that it required cohesion and tradition. The elders worked to keep the old systems and the old pattern of authority in place, as much as that was possible in the midst of a world that had just turned upside down.

Priests

Many of the priests also went into exile, along with the royalty, the politicians, and the local village elders. However, most of the local priests stayed behind in Judah, where they conducted worship on the high places of each village and among the ruins of the Jerusalem temple. Still, many priests became exiles in the new land of Babylonia. Probably the priests who went to Babylonia were the ones who had ministered at the temple in Jerusalem. These included the high priest and others who were in charge of Judah's national bureaucracy. In the ancient world, priests often served as governmental bureaucrats, and so there may have been a large number of former priests in the city of Babylon itself.

Not all priests in Judah had focused their attentions on the Jerusalem temple, however. Many of them lived throughout the country, ministering in the outlying towns, the villages, and in the rural areas. These lower-level priests were transplanted along with their local village elders to the area around Nippur. Earlier in their lives, these priests had ministered to the people in their areas. They spent their time offering the sacrifices of the locals, but invested most of their energy in teaching people about the faith. Down by the riverside around Nippur, the priests lived and worked the land for their daily bread, and on the Sabbaths, they gathered there by the river to remember their lost Promised Land. Because of their need to labor, they limited their teaching activities to those public occasions, but the transmission of the ancient traditions to the next generations still occupied their time and their interest.

Perhaps the priests had the hardest time of any of these people in their adjustment to a new land. Their daily activities were greatly changed. It may be even more important that these priests were without a temple. Even the priests who had ministered in the outlying regions of Judah knew the importance of the central temple in Jerusalem. That was the special place where God caused the divine name to dwell, where God was present in a special way as nowhere else in the world. With the temple utterly destroyed, how could the priests hope that God could be nearby, or that they could reach God at all through their prayers and offerings? Perhaps the priests even wondered in quiet whispers if God was still alive. After all, the Babylonian armies had destroyed God's home and laid it in ruins; they had even taken all the furnishings right out from the middle of the temple and carted them off wholesale to Babylon. How could God stand that? Why did God not do anything about it?

The priests knew better than anyone the ancient stories about God's deliverance of the people. Yahweh could turn the sea into dry land, could control the weather, and could defeat any earthly army. But when Babylonia seized Jerusalem, God did nothing. Perhaps God was no longer alive. Perhaps there was no longer any reason to be a priest of Yahweh. I suspect that many Jerusalem priests became servants of one of the

Babylonian gods, searching after a god who could win and whose life was visible in the might of the army and the wealth of the nation. Certainly, over the centuries, there have been many priests and ministers who have chased after power and wealth, thinking that they find God there. But many of the priests stayed faithful, such as they could when there was no temple. They taught, they prayed, they read their scriptures and wrote about their experiences, they made offerings to God in places by the river. Most importantly, they gathered the people together and made sure that they remembered their faith. Even though the priests struggled to hold onto the shreds of their former faith, they recognized within each other and within themselves the need for a faith in the one true and ancient God that included their new situation. They needed a faith for a new day, and this search kept the priests quite busy, and often quite frustrated as well.

Suffering

As all of these rulers, government officials, village elders, priests, and others gathered together in Babylonia, their life was not prosperous, but was not a life of poverty or oppression. Still, their new life represented a huge change from the life that they lived in Judah. Their new life may have been comfortable economically, but they had been the wealthiest of their country, and now they could see the amazing wealth of others in the capital of the world. Their pain was greatest in watching the advantages of others and remembering how much better their own life had been. When the exiles gathered together, their memories often turned to their past glory and to the suffering of their current way of life. Some of these sufferings found expression in the Bible's psalms.

> By the rivers of Babylonia,
>   there we sat,
>   and how we wept when we remembered Zion.
> Into the midst of the willows
>   we retired our harps.

For there our captors asked us for songs,
    and our tormentors asked for joy:
"Sing us one of the songs of Zion!"

How can we sing Yahweh's song on foreign soil?
If I forget you, O Jerusalem,
    let my right hand wither!
Let my tongue cling to the roof of my mouth
    if I do not remember you,
    if I do not lift Jerusalem
        above my highest joy.

Psalm 137:1–6[9]

With psalms like these, the exiles bemoaned their fate. Though they had enough to eat, they felt homeless and abandoned. The Jews felt separated from their God, whom they thought still lived in Jerusalem, far away. God was too far to hear them or to bind them together, and they cried out their loss. Without their faith, who were they? So they pledged to remember Jerusalem, to hold onto their faith and their previous way of life. They would not forget the years when God was with them, when they were God's chosen ones, living in privilege. Together, many of the exiles promised that Babylonia would not be their home, only the place where they stayed for a while. They agreed to disagree with the culture around them and to yearn for the place of the old days. The more they strove to hold onto their past, the more they perceived their current situation as homelessness and hopelessness, as true suffering.

Ezekiel the Exile

Ezekiel was one of the younger priests in exile. His memories of Jerusalem were fresh in his mind, and they were memories of youth. He had almost completed the lengthy apprenticeship for the priesthood when the Babylonians took him

---

[9] All scriptural quotations are the author's translation or paraphrase.

into exile. For all of his life, Ezekiel had struggled to learn the secrets of the temple and to find acceptance in the tightly knit circle of priests. It was the dream of his life to offer the sacrifices and to pronounce the sacred words of faith. But the exile shattered those dreams just as they were about to come true. To the frustrations of all the priests, Ezekiel added the abject disappointment of failing to attain his lifelong goal at the very moment in which he expected to achieve it.

In order to understand Ezekiel, it is essential to think of him as an exile. He wanted to be a priest with all of his soul, but the Babylonian army took that all away from him. He spent the rest of his life searching for ways to serve God in a strange land, a place that never felt right to him no matter how well he came to know it. He clearly knew who had won that war; Babylonia was the victor, and Ezekiel sensed the futility of trying to copy the old faith in a new world. He struggled to hold onto the core of faith while finding the right ways to express it in a new land, as a minority people, without the temple where God had always lived.

Meetings at the River

Ezekiel met with the other Jewish exiles at the banks of a river each week. They gathered to remember their former life, but Ezekiel knew that mere memory would never be enough to bring their ancient faith into the new world. God needed to find a way to be with the exiles in the distant land of Babylonia. Could God find a way to travel the distance? Could the Jews find a way to worship God as a minority in the Babylonian Empire instead of as rulers of their own land? Could their faith survive the sudden expansion of the exiles' worldview? Each week, down by the riverside, Ezekiel struggled with these questions, and in response he found a way to transform the religion that he had learned as a child into a new and deeper faith that could survive the challenges of their present and their future. The echoes of that newly energized faith resound throughout this prophet's book.

2

A Chariot of Fire

(Ezekiel 1)

The book of Ezekiel begins with a strange vision, full of chariots and fire, living creatures with wings and too many faces, and a throne floating through the air. Lightning flashes and objects soar in the sky. Ezekiel's vision goes far beyond our normal, everyday experiences. Our modern attempts to understand this vision run the gamut from songs such as "Ezekiel Saw de Wheel," which repeat Ezekiel's own words, to strained speculations about extraterrestrial beings in ancient UFOs, which reflect our own uncertainty that the event can find an explanation in terms sensible to us moderns. But certainly we can add explanation to our repetition of this vision without wandering too far from the importance of what this story says.

So how do we explain Ezekiel's odd vision? Was this some vast intervention of God into the natural world? Did Ezekiel hallucinate an apparition of God, possibly under the influence of some psychotropic mind-altering substance? Neither extreme of explanation proves satisfying to all interpreters. Perhaps such explanations are really attempts to *explain away* the vision rather than dealing with its strange content. Visions are things seen, later to be described. What is important about a vision is not the external visual stimuli that start it. Visionaries are people who perceive events—maybe the same events that every other person sees—but who perceive a deeper meaning behind it. For an example, consider the example of Amos, another prophet who saw visions (Amos 7:1—8:3). Amos sees everyday things—insects, construction materials, baskets of fruit. But he doesn't just see the objects themselves; after all, anyone could do that. The visionary prophet Amos understands each of these objects as a symbol for some deeper part of God's reality. It takes no special revelation to be a visionary; it takes special insight to perceive and comprehend the visions that everyone sees every day. We don't know what Ezekiel saw, and it probably isn't all that important. Seeing isn't believing, and what is vital about Ezekiel's writing is his belief—not any magically flying objects. His knowledge of God, expressed to us through visions, lasts longer and affects us more deeply than one ancient person's mystical experiences.

No matter how we explain the first chapter of Ezekiel, this is obviously a vision of great power. Things happen in this vision that do not happen every day. Ezekiel describes things far beyond the limits of "normal" life. The event is supernatural, extraordinary, and telling about it leads the storyteller into the surprising, through the bizarre and the unpredictable, right up to the border of the incredulous and the absurd.

But the story begins in simple, straightforward, natural tones. On a certain day, Ezekiel was sitting on the riverbank (Ezekiel 1:1–3). It was the Chebar River, a small canal that ran not far from the city of Nippur, probably flowing into the Euphrates River before it went much farther. It seems that the Chebar was not one of the popular gathering places for the exiled Jews, perhaps because it was a bit too far away from the populated parts of Nippur for many people to go there often.

Ezekiel had gone to the Chebar to be alone, and alone he was. Sitting on the banks of that small canal, thinking to himself, his mind wandered to the same things to which it always returned. Ezekiel the almost-priest in a foreign land thought about the God whom he had left behind in Jerusalem when the Babylonian army forced Jews to march to this new place. Was God still there? Did God care about the Jews in exile, or had God forsaken them? Could they ever be close to God again? What could the exiles believe about God?

And as Ezekiel sat alone on the banks of the river Chebar, he was no longer alone, and his answers came to him.

Wheels Within Wheels

Through the lens of vision and imagination, Ezekiel saw something nearly indescribable. It begins as a fierce storm, blown on a powerful wind (1:4). Babylonia is a flat country. Just as in the flat territory of the United States' Great Plains, powerful storms can blow up very fast with almost no warning. Ezekiel had surely been in Babylonia long enough to have seen clouds like this before; he knew the vicious thunderstorms that would soon be upon him if the clouds moved his way. He watched for awhile as the dark cloud grew on the horizon, to see which way it would go. This cloud grew faster than most did, and it seemed to be coming right at him. Even at a great distance, he could see the lightning flashing inside it. It would be a bad storm, even worse than most of the sudden thunderstorms in that region.

But as the storm came closer, Ezekiel began to notice strange things about it. There was something in the middle of the cloud. It was a yellowish glow, and in its center was an object. Though anyone else would have run for cover with such a severe storm approaching, Ezekiel stood right where he was, entranced by the sight of what was approaching, and as it drew closer, he could distinguish more and more of the thing inside the lightning storm. Ezekiel started his description at the bottom of the apparition, where there were four living creatures and four matching wheels. The living creatures looked human, but they were far from being human; whatever they really were has never been seen again. Each living creature had four wings and four faces. Their feet were hooves set above wheels like jewels. Each of the creatures faced a different direction, and each had faces set in every direction: a human face, a lion's face, an ox's face, and an eagle's face. The whole contraption moved as one piece, in any direction that it desired without turning, and there were flashes of lightning within its midst (1:4–21).

On top of these living creatures and their wheels was a platform. As Ezekiel saw the platform, he began to realize that the creatures and their wheels formed a vehicle to transport whatever was on the platform. With a great sound like mighty thunder, like crashing waters, the creatures flew, taking the dome-shaped crystal platform anywhere it would go (1:22–25). There was a throne on that platform, and on the throne, surrounded by glowing light and flashes of even greater brightness, was "an image like an appearance of a human form" (1:26).[1] Around this human-like form was a rainbow, set in the midst of this huge dark cloud.

Ezekiel saw all of this and responded with a confession of deepest faith: "This was the appearance of the likeness of the glory of Yahweh" (1:28). It was God! God sat on the throne, borne by this fantastic conveyance, surrounded by gleaming brightness and darkest clouds, traveling from the north to approach Ezekiel on the banks of the small river Chebar. And when he realized that this was God, come across the vast emptiness from Jerusalem's shattered temple to stand right at his feet, Ezekiel fell to the ground and worshiped.

A Vision Beyond Words

Through all the description of this indescribable vision, Ezekiel's tongue kept tripping over itself. He searched for

---

[1] The image has similarities to other biblical depictions of God's throne and the altar of God in the temple.

words to describe what he saw, but he didn't know the words. He kept groping at phrases such as "it looked like" this or "it had an appearance like" that. At the conclusion, when Ezekiel realized what he saw, he still could not find words that described the exact vision, so he relied on grand indirection: "This was the appearance of the likeness of the glory of Yahweh" (1:28). He didn't even insist that God was there, and certainly he did not suggest that he himself actually *saw* God. God's glory looked something like this thing in the sky, but all that Ezekiel saw was something that appeared like an image of God's glory. What exactly did he see? It's hard for us to tell, because it's hard for Ezekiel to tell.

This grasping for the right words makes it very difficult for us to read his description and to envision the same things that he saw. Fortunately, the object itself isn't the point of the vision. When we read the story, we should not try to figure out the structural design of this flying object. Instead, Ezekiel's point is quite different, and his point comes through the story even when we do not understand exactly what he saw. The meaning is the important thing; the experiences that triggered the understanding fade into insignificance.

When Ezekiel saw the fantastic vision, only one thing came to his mind: *God moves.* That was the most urgent thing to him; the reason for this miraculous vision was much more important than the form it took. Ezekiel, like all the other priests who found themselves in Babylonian exile, was continually asking himself if God could possibly be with them in exile. Then Ezekiel saw God on the move, sitting on a miraculous, divine, indescribable throne and traveling through the skies on some magnificent chariot. The devout questioner met the surprising answer face to face on the banks of a river.

For Ezekiel, there are three questions addressed by this vision. The first question is "What about the temple?" God had dwelled in the temple for three hundred years, and as far as anyone knew, God had never left it in all that time. Could God survive without that Jerusalem temple? Secondly, what's God doing in a chariot? What does it mean that God would choose this kind of conveyance? The final question wonders who leads whom. Is God really following the people?

What About the Temple?

Can God live without a temple? It seems almost a silly question for us today, since we believe that God is not limited to physical places. God is spirit, we fondly say, and has no need of buildings. But the ancient traditions insisted that God had chosen to live in the Jerusalem temple, which Solomon had built. God had lived there for three centuries, after all, and that was certainly long enough to prove something. For these Jews, God lived in the temple not so much because God *needed* a temple, but because God *chose* a temple. In the old days, God lived in a tent and moved freely with the people; in Moses' day God had even lived in a cloud by day and a fire by night. God could live wherever God so chose; the Jews knew that and to them, that was precisely the point. God had chosen to live in the temple, and now the temple was gone. What would God choose next?

According to the old stories, it was King David who had first wanted to build a temple for God, but God said no. God would build a house, a dynasty, for David, instead of David building a house of cedar, a temple, for God (2 Samuel 7). But God announced at that point that the next king would build the temple.[2] When King Solomon came to power, he very quickly set about building a grand temple, using forced labor from throughout his kingdom and purchasing the highest quality building materials from throughout the known world. The temple construction took seven years, and once it was finished, Solomon started work on building his own palace, which took thirteen years to complete, built to a scale that would dwarf the temple of God (1 Kings 6—8).

---

[2] Quite possibly, 2 Samuel 7 was written during or after Solomon's time to explain why it was acceptable for Solomon to build a temple when David had chosen not to do so.

When all the construction was finally complete, Solomon dedicated the temple in a fabulous ceremony. All the priests, Levites, and elders assembled from throughout the kingdom, and they marched in a long procession into the temple courts, carrying the Ark of the Covenant with the two tablets of the Ten Commandments. The climax of the dedication ceremony came when the priests carried the Ark into the middle of the holy place within the temple.

> When the priests came out of the holy place, a cloud filled the house of Yahweh, so the priests were not able to stand up in order to minister in front of the cloud; for Yahweh's glory filled Yahweh's house. Then Solomon said, "Yahweh has agreed to dwell in thick darkness. I have built you an exalted house, a place for you to dwell in forever."
>
> 1 Kings 8:10–13

Though Yahweh could live anywhere, God had promised to live in the deep darkness in the middle of the temple. The creator of sun and stars would forsake the lights of the skies and the distant heavens to inhabit the thick smoke and gloom in the center of Solomon's construction. Israel's early writers sensed the disturbing contradiction in this act, and so they quote Solomon again:

> "But will God indeed dwell on the earth? Even heaven and the highest heaven cannot contain you, much less this house that I have built! Regard your servant's prayer and his plea, O Yahweh my God, hearing the cry and the prayer that your servant prays to you today; that your eyes may be open night and day toward this house, toward the place of which you said, 'My name shall be there,' that you may heed the prayer that your servant prays toward this place."
>
> 1 Kings 8:27–29

Though Solomon knew that Yahweh was too big for a temple, he still insisted that God had a special connection to this one physical place. God's presence was grounded in promise. God would be at the temple constantly not because God required a temple but because God had promised to be there and to hear the prayers uttered in the temple. This tradition grew to great importance in Israel's history. Without the temple, one could never be positive that God would grant favorable answers to human prayer. The temple became the guarantee of human prayer; if there was no temple, anyone who prayed took a chance, since one could never be sure if God was there to hear the prayer.

Another issue on Ezekiel's mind was the Promised Land. Yahweh had chosen to be the God of the Israelites, and God brought the people out of Egypt to live in that land. Would God pay any attention to those who lived outside that land? Most people of the ancient world would have said no. The common perception was that every nation and every land had its own deity. Yahweh was the Israelites' god, in just the same way that Marduk was the Babylonian god, Baal was the Canaanite god, and so forth. Now that the Jews were outside of Israel and Judah, would Yahweh pay any attention to them?

For Ezekiel, the answer was that *God moves*. God is not limited to temple or to land. God's connection is to the people, and God will move wherever they do. Just as God had dwelled in thick dark smoke in Jerusalem's temple, God now moves through the air in the midst of a dark cloud. The exile in no way came between God and God's people, because God could leave Jerusalem at any time, and would do so in order to be with the chosen people. This thought was shockingly new, and it was both comforting and threatening. It was comforting because it assured Ezekiel for the first time that God would be present with the Babylonian exiles. They would not be forced to spend their lives without God, because God moves. But it was threatening, too. Gods who live in temples are predictable and stable; one can always find God when the need arises. But a God who moves can't be controlled or predicted. More than that, God's moving violates the old traditions that insist on God's presence in the temple. Ezekiel sees a frighteningly independent God who moves despite what everyone believed of God.

Can God live without a temple, in any land of God's choosing? It's a most important question for us today. We go to our church buildings to find God, and sometimes we forget that God can move. We assume God's presence at all times, taking God for granted as much as Israel's kings had done. We think that we know God and that God won't change, but God violates the expectations of God's people over and over again. We think that God's voice is heard today in the same places as ever, and sometimes we don't stop to hear God's voice coming from new places. God speaks in the temple but God also speaks on the banks of the river, and today God speaks in churches and outside them, too, throughout the world. God moves, and often shows up where we least expect to see and hear God.

What's God Doing in a Chariot?

God had lived for three centuries in the middle of dark smoke, safely nestled in the heart of Jerusalem's temple, but now God moves through the air in the middle of a dark cloud, cruising through the skies on the way from Jerusalem to join the exiles in the land of Babylonia. But God is not alone in that cloud. Yahweh rides the clouds on a fancy, fiery chariot, with mystical, magical living creatures surrounding by flashing lights and gleaming glows of brightness. Why does God need this kind of apparatus?

What Ezekiel sees certainly seems odd to us, but his contemporaries would have recognized it instantly, in generality if not in all of its specifics. Ezekiel draws on elements of a very different religious tradition than what the Bible normally contains. In many other nations of the ancient Near East, religions focused on idols and images of the gods. The later traditions of the Old Testament were very much against any worship involving idols, and they understood the worship of Yahweh to be very different from the other religions where idols were more commonly accepted. However, most ancient people knew that their god was not the idol itself. Instead, the idol was an important representation of the deity; it might even have been a place where the deity lived or at least visited frequently. For this reason, the worshipers treated their images with great respect. Idols took central place in the shrines, and the people directed their worship toward the idol, not because it *was* their god but because it *reminded* them of their god.

In much the same way, most of today's Christian churches place a cross in the center of the chancel, so that it becomes the focus of the worshipers' attention. The congregation faces the cross and sings its songs of praise in its direction, but without thinking that the cross *is* our God; it is only a reminder of Jesus Christ. We do not worship the cross, but we treat it with respect and give it pride of place within our worship services, in much the same way that ancient peoples treated their idols.

Ancient idol worship went farther than that, however. In the wealth of our modern society and churches, every sanctuary can afford at least one cross (even if it is only brown-painted styrofoam), and some congregations spend huge sums of money on numerous expensive crosses of beautiful wood, metal, or even crystal. In ancient times, the skill required to craft one of these ornate images was so great that there were very few of them. This made it much easier for people to identify God with the object. We have seen so many crosses that we know none of them is the "real" place of Christ, but if we had only seen one of them in our entire life, then we would much more likely think that Jesus was somehow associated with that one particular cross. The image would move from being a symbolic reminder to functioning as the presumed location of the deity.

The ancients had relatively few images, but they understood their gods to be present within those images in special ways. But at times, the people would worship the god in a different place, and so they would move the image to the new location for worship. The movement of the gods often required special vehicles, and there are many descriptions in the ancient Near East of the transport of gods in fancy chariots pulled by animals or, more frequently, carried on pallets by human worshipers. When the Babylonian army conquered Jerusalem and formed huge caravans to cart off the city's wealth to Babylonia, the artifacts of the temple rode in chariots like these, and the Jews would have seen how their temple vessels moved from one nation to another in these sorts of conveyances, just as the gods of all the other nations moved around.

When Ezekiel describes God's movement in the clouds from Jerusalem to Babylonia, Yahweh's conveyance is very similar to these transports of other ancient Near Eastern gods. At one level, this should not be too surprising. After all, the Ark of the Covenant was not too different from these other gods' vehicles (1 Samuel 4—6; 2 Samuel 6). In the old days, Yahweh had ridden to battle in such a contraption, and now in another age it happens again. But in those intervening centuries, it became less common for Israelites to depict their God in ways similar to other nations' deities.

Ezekiel commits a scandal when he claims that Yahweh moves around in the same type of vehicle that all the other gods do. It removes much of the distance between Yahweh and these other so-called gods; it makes them seem all alike, a theological move that would have seemed all the more dangerous as different ideas surrounded the exiles. But that simply underscores the inventiveness and the daring of Ezekiel's prophecy. Not only was he willing to violate the ancient, sacred traditions of Yahweh's dwelling in the center of the Jerusalem temple, he was willing to show God on the move in ways similar to how other gods moved. Ezekiel's attempts to find new answers to urgent theological questions took him in quite unexpected directions, and so he describes a God who does the unexpected, including using the same transportation as pagan deities. It is not so much the manner of God's action, but the very fact that God does act: God moves.

Who's Leading Whom?

Throughout the early years, when God and the people (then under Moses' direction) wandered through the wilderness for forty years, God always stayed in front of the people, in a cloud by day and a fire by night. In this way, God was in the lead, and by leading Moses, God was able to lead the whole people. It was always perfectly clear that God knew where the people should go, and that God would guide them there, in God's own time. But this scene in Ezekiel 1 paints a different picture. The Babylonians took the Jews from their homeland and brought them to places like Nippur, near the river Chebar. Then God came to where the exiles were. It seems as if the people led God out of Jerusalem and into a new land.

Of course, humans do not determine or control divine action. Ezekiel's vision emphasizes the fierce independence of God. No one drives Yahweh's chariot. Instead, Ezekiel keeps repeating that it goes wherever the *ru'ach* goes (1:12, 20, 21). The Hebrew word *ru'ach* is difficult to translate into English, because it can mean "wind," "breath," or "spirit." In Ezekiel 1, most translations render it as "spirit," with the sense that God's spirit directly controls the vehicle. This interpretation of *ru'ach* emphasizes the point quite well: God controls the chariot, and it takes God in the direction God desires. No one forces God to go anywhere. God appears in Babylonia not because God *needs* the Jews but because God *chooses* to be present with them. The Jews have not led God to Babylonia; only God leads God.

But an insistence on divine autonomy misses the point somewhat. This chapter's purpose is not to assert divine independence. Ezekiel shows the reader God's overarching desire to be with the chosen people. In this portrait, God feels for the Jews and suffers with them and for them in their exile.[3] God bridges the gulf and joins the people in their time of need. This is a sensitive, caring God who is motivated to care for the people. Whether the divine nature requires human contact or not, this God yearns to be with the people and will not rest

---

[3] By this thinking, it seems inevitable that God also suffered with the people who still lived in Jerusalem, but Ezekiel does not understand this. He sees a God who comes to him personally, leaving others behind to do so.

until God is in the midst of the faithful community. No distance is too great to cover and no pain is too great for God to endure in order to be with the exiles. God is self-motivated and cannot be controlled by any person or any group, but deep inside, on a most intense emotional level, the exiles' plight moves God, and thus God moves.

Surprises by the River

While sitting on the bank of the river Chebar, Ezekiel receives quite a surprise. He gains a vision of God, and God moves to Babylonia to take up a new residence with the people. When God moves, God surprises the exiles. Firstly, the move is surprising because God leaves the temple, where Yahweh had lived for three centuries. Secondly, it surprises because Yahweh travels just like the other ancient gods did. Lastly, it is surprising that God decides to leave the land of the ancestors to follow the people; for Yahweh, people are more important than land.

Temples could not contain Yahweh, and theological ideas could not control God, either. God even violated the most central, treasured theologies, such as the centrality of the temple in worship, the connection with the land, and the dissimilarity between God and other gods. For Yahweh, theology and theological rightness are not as important as presence with the people. This proves quite surprising to priests of every age.

Such a vision was terrifying and exciting for Ezekiel, and it excites and challenges us just as much today. These surprises by the river would shock and disturb us. We long for a predictable, controllable God, who plays by simple rules that we can understand. We want temples (or worship services or theologies) where we can be sure that we will find God. We want a path to salvation that we can count on, as if God will dispense our reward if we just jump through the right hoops. But Yahweh frustrates all expectations. God is faithful and loyal, but not predictable or controllable. This is frightening, but it frees God to react to human suffering in any way necessary.

We keep trying to trap God in a box, whether through the physical limits of a church building where we're sure that God comes to us in a special way or through the theological definitions that we contrive as certain, fundamental, or essential to life with God. But at the root, nothing is essential to life with God except life with God, and that life is much more subject to God's own choice than to ours. Ezekiel's vision emphasizes that profound moment of faith, when the believer has spent a lifetime of preparation only to confront the fact that it is God who comes, it is God who saves, and it is God who moves.

3

Speaking Without Words

(Ezekiel 2—6, 12)

Prophets have a message to share with God's people. But once they know the message, they face a problem: *how* do they tell this message? What words do they choose? How do they select their audience, and how do they know the right time to speak? What tone of voice should they use? The different prophets answered these questions in different ways. Some spoke in long speeches; others uttered short, cryptic sayings. Some used poetry; some spoke in prose. Amos borrowed the style used in denunciations of foreign nations, Hosea referred to the terminology of the fertility religions, Jeremiah shouted harsh accusations at God, and Malachi recorded his prophecy as an argument between proponents of different views. Each method of speech was different, but all served the same function, because all the prophets chose forms of speech that would make their message heard more clearly by their chosen audience.

Much of Ezekiel's prophesying came in the form of sign-acts. Sign-acts are a peculiar form where words join with striking actions to make one unified statement. Jesus performed a sign-act after the resurrection, according to the Gospel of John. In one of the post-resurrection appearances, Jesus approached the disciples and blew his breath on each one of them, saying, "Receive the holy spirit" (John 20:22). The Greek word *pneuma*, like the Hebrew word *ru'ach*, can mean wind, breath, or spirit. Jesus blew his *pneuma* on the disciples and told them to receive the holy *pneuma*. The action (blowing *breath*) and the words ("receive the *spirit*") reinforce the meaning of each other in the minds of the audience. Because learning can take place through watching and through listening, sign-acts make very effective teaching techniques. The message and the means of expressing that message combine and strengthen each other.

Ezekiel used a wide variety of prophetic sign-acts. The prophet ate scrolls, built toy walls and broke them down, laid on his side for years with little food, and shaved his beard so that he could weigh the results. Such behavior was strange, to say the least. In all probability, anyone seeing Ezekiel would have thought him odd, if not deranged. Ezekiel has often been described as psychotic because of these sign-acts.

This prophet was a shrewd communicator of the Word, however. He attracted people's attention in whatever way worked, and he made his message clear in the midst of it all. Sign-acts would get attention. The word of such events would spread throughout the community like wildfire: "Did you hear what that Ezekiel did today?" Everyone wanted to gossip about this strange prophet and his weird acts. Inevitably, everyone soon knew what he was doing, and just as inevitably came the hard questions. People wanted to know *why*. Why did Ezekiel lie on his side all day? Once people asked the questions, then the prophet had them hooked. The answers spread, too, and soon everyone knew what the prophet wanted them to know. They may not agree at all, but the message has been sent and the people have received it loud and clear. When the audience saw these sign-acts, they could not help but comprehend Ezekiel's message. Ezekiel's message fit best into sign-acts, perhaps, because it was a message of the unspeakable: the destruction of Jerusalem, and all that the religious establishment has held dear. Ezekiel spoke to the exiles in Babylonia, and quite possibly most of them had been gone long before the destruction of Jerusalem had actually occurred. When they left their home city, they had seen the fancy buildings still standing, with the walls surrounding them mostly intact. But a decade later the Babylonian army leveled the city, and Ezekiel kept reminding them that their beloved homeland was gone, demolished, destroyed. The people did not want to hear such horrifying news, but Ezekiel kept nagging them until they had no place to hide from the reality. Jerusalem had been destroyed, and there was no more home to which they could ever return. Once the people realized that they could not go home to Jerusalem again, then they could begin to accept the new life in exile, and Ezekiel knew from his vision that exilic life *could* be life with God.

Eating the Scroll (2:8—3:3)

When Yahweh appeared to Ezekiel in the terrifyingly unexpected opening vision, Yahweh approached the prophet, wishing to speak. God commanded him to rise, and a spirit filled Ezekiel so that he could stand up in God's presence. Then, Yahweh commissioned Ezekiel to speak to Israel, which was a rebellious people. God cautioned Ezekiel that many of the people would refuse to hear, but that Ezekiel must speak forth God's message anyway. Then, God gave Ezekiel the message. The message came in the form of a scroll, delivered by God's own hand. Ezekiel swallowed the scroll, which had words written on it both front and back.

Ezekiel never tells us exactly what the scroll said, but he summarizes its contents: the words are words of lamentation, mourning, and woe (2:10). Ezekiel fills himself with these negative words, and this bad news nourishes his prophecy from that day forth. Out of this stomach-full of depressing negativity comes all of his words in the rest of the book. Yet Ezekiel claims that the scroll tasted as sweet as honey (3:3). The scroll with bitter words tastes sweet to this prophet. This paradox sets in motion the dynamic that will dominate the sign-acts and most of the book: the prophet is quite contrary. He dedicates his life to announcing God's presence, which gives meaning and purpose to Ezekiel's life, but the presence of God will not make the people happy.[1]

For Ezekiel's mission is to afflict the people with divine truth, announcing their responsibility and depicting the destruction at hand. If there is hope in Ezekiel's message, it will not be apparent for many chapters to come. Through this sign-act, Ezekiel makes his point in a very vivid way. Sign-acts were probably not performed only once; Ezekiel would have re-enacted this event repeatedly for different audiences, so that everyone could see exactly what he meant. When his audiences saw him smile with the sweetness of some bitter scrap, they would know that they dealt with a strange person whose messages from God would seem quite perverse.

Interlude: The Watcher (3:16–21)

A week after his initial vision, Ezekiel hears God again, and this time God explains the prophet's task in greater detail: "I have appointed you to be a watcher for the house of Israel" (3:17). Ezekiel's job is to listen to God's messages and to watch the signs of the times, and then to warn the people about what they are doing. This is not prediction; God does not want Ezekiel to announce *future* events before they happen. Instead, God tells Ezekiel to describe to people what they are doing at the moment. If someone sins, Ezekiel must boldly proclaim that sin. For the prophet, this is a life and death issue, because

---

[1] This same dynamic appears other times that God calls prophets, such as Jeremiah 1 (especially verses 10, 16–19) and Isaiah 6:9–10.

God will hold him responsible for the acts of others. This is the first glimmer of Ezekiel's advanced notion of responsibility, which will appear frequently throughout the book. For now, the book emphasizes Ezekiel's task of stating reality, of telling people exactly what they are doing right and what they are doing wrong.

As watcher, Ezekiel is to live on the outside of the community. He should see everything that happens, but he himself should not participate. Like a priest, his life is to be separate from the rest of the people. This distance is awkward for Ezekiel, but it defines his task and his self. Throughout the rest of these sign-acts, the reader realizes over and over again how different Ezekiel is. Certainly, the prophet is not a role model for the other people of faith; his very life functions as a sign, pointing to God's reality that the people should see and learn.

Silence (3:22–27)

Another sign-act follows immediately after the description of Ezekiel as watcher. Yahweh commands Ezekiel to go to his house, where he will be tied up so that he cannot move. Then God commands Ezekiel to be silent. Immediately after God charges Ezekiel with the responsibility to describe to the people their faults, God tells the prophet to keep quiet. Ezekiel should speak only when God speaks to him, and then the prophet should start his utterances with the formula, "Thus says Yahweh God." In this way, all the exiles will know that everything Ezekiel says is a word from God; they should not disregard anything that the prophet says.

This sign-act encourages the people to pay very close attention to Ezekiel's few statements. All extraneous conversation disappears, and suddenly every word draws attention and receives new meaning. But this situation creates an eerie aura around this prophet. Each word carries so much importance, and yet the prophet is almost always silent. People around him wait for the special word to come, but usually they receive only dead silence from a prophet who sits by himself, tied up in his own house. The starkness of the scene sends chills through the spine. Here is God's message to the people, cast in human form, so close that people could touch it, but the only message they hear is silence. Even when God comes into Babylonia, even when God comes close to the people, God is still so strangely distant.

The Brick and the Wall (4:1–3)

Ezekiel then undertakes a complex sign-act to symbolize Jerusalem's destruction. The prophet was performing these sign-acts around the year 593 B.C.E., about four years after these exiles had arrived in Babylonia, but six or seven years before the final devastation of Jerusalem.[2] When Ezekiel discusses the fall of Jerusalem in these early sign-acts, he tries to convince his listeners about an event that he thinks is inevitable, but that they wish to ignore. The Babylonian Empire would not be satisfied until Jerusalem was completely removed as a city that could one day regain its prominence. Their armies would not stop until they had flattened Jerusalem and its buildings, but the Jewish exiles in Babylonia still maintained hope that their home would be safe, so that someday they could return there. Ezekiel crushes that hope repeatedly and mercilessly.

As a sign-act, Ezekiel follows Yahweh's orders to take a brick and to sketch Jerusalem on it. The prophet then played war with that brick, besieging it and shouting at it (4:1–3, 7). This play-acting represents God's desire that Jerusalem receive what it deserves for its wrongdoing. The actions that Babylonia would soon take against Jerusalem were inevitable, and God would not stop it.

In this section, Ezekiel comes closest to stating plainly his thought that Jerusalem's destruction was inevitable. Most of the signs that follow in the next several chapters of Ezekiel's

---

[2] For dates, see Moshe Greenberg, *Ezekiel 1—20* (Anchor Bible 22; Garden City, New York: Doubleday, 1983), pp. 7–11.

book repeat this same point in a variety of ways. But the point is clear: Jerusalem is about to be destroyed, and nothing can stop it. This message would have devastated the exiles' hopes for a quick return. But for Ezekiel, this is good news of a strange sort, because it shows that God will stay in Babylonia with the exiles, in a new and permanent home there.

Being One-sided (4:4–17)

As the sign-act of the besieged brick continues, Ezekiel lies on his left side for three hundred ninety days, and then on his right for forty days. These correspond to the nations of Israel and Judah, respectively. In our modern thinking, the direction toward the top (or straight ahead) on a map is north, but for the ancients, the first direction was toward the rising sun, in the east. Standing in the middle of Israel and Judah, facing east, Judah would be on one's right and Israel on one's left. When Ezekiel lies on his left side, it represents Israel, and the three hundred ninety days on that side would indicate the years of Israel's sin (4:5). Judah receives a shorter sentence, only forty years, and so Ezekiel spends only forty days on his right side.

Despite many attempts to correlate these figures to historical periods, no one correspondence seems to make sense. At best, these numbers represent a comparison. The Babylonian exiles have come from Judah, and they now hear from the prophet that there will be harsh punishment because of their nation's sins. But there is a distinct note of hope: the punishment will be only about one-tenth that of the northern nation of Israel. At this point, Israel would have been destroyed for about one hundred thirty years, and there was still no sign at all that they would ever be restored. For these Judean exiles, there was hope. They had to wait a much shorter time before their punishment would be over. Though specific dates cannot be determined, the passage presents the general sense that Judah's time of punishment would be short and, more importantly, would be survivable. If they could not avoid their punishment, at least they could have hopes of rebuilding afterwards. But the destruction would come first.

Even in the midst of such seriousness, humor is not completely absent. Ezekiel's priestly scruples are fully intact, and so he is willing to argue with God. God insists that Ezekiel lie on his side, without getting up to find and cook food. God even suggests that Ezekiel burn his own human waste as fuel to cook his food. Ezekiel knows that this would violate God's own law, since it would make the food ritually unclean, and so Ezekiel negotiates for an exception. God grants the request, and allows Ezekiel to cook with cow dung instead of human dung. The sight is still ridiculous; Ezekiel cooks his food just a few inches in front of his face, since he cannot reach very far away. The cow must have deposited the dung close at hand.

Yet the deep seriousness of the passage is never far away. Stretching Ezekiel beyond his ability to believe, God orders the prophet to violate God's own law. Ezekiel does not allow this to happen, but God's willingness to give that command hangs in the air like thick smoke. Just as in the inaugural vision, when God left home, broke the promises to live in Jerusalem forever, and rode into Babylonia on a conveyance such as that used by other, pagan gods, God does the unexpected. God is willing to break all the rules, including the laws that God had commanded, in order to share presence and message with the exiles. This kind of God is thoroughly unpredictable.

A Close Shave (5:1–17)

The next sign-act requires Ezekiel to shave off completely the hair from his face and his head. Then, Ezekiel takes the pile of hair and separates it into thirds. He burns a third of his hair, causing an awful stench, to symbolize the burning of Jerusalem. He strikes the second third with a sword, reminding the people of the type of death that the Jerusalemites would suffer if they fled the burning city into the traps of the waiting Babylonian army. Ezekiel scatters the final third to the wind, and some of them also burn, representing the fact that death still awaited some of the exiles who had scattered into the ends of the known world.

Later, Ezekiel describes some of the greatest horrors of Jerusalem's siege. As the food supply dwindles into nonexistence, the people resort to cannibalism, eating their own relatives in order to keep part of the family alive. Famine would perhaps claim the most victims in its slow death. Swarms of starving rodents and insects would take others, and the sword would await the rest. God's word is final, and Jerusalem's destruction is assured.

Prophesying to the Mountains (6:1–10)

Ezekiel now starts to yell his prophecies to the mountains and valleys around him, in a sign-act that would have seemed sheer lunacy to those observing this prophet. In this sign-act, the destruction of Jerusalem spreads from the city itself to the surrounding countryside. The sword flashes on the hills around the city, bringing the same end to the rural folk nearby. Even those people who could escape Jerusalem could not avoid its fate. Even if the exiles could return to be near Jerusalem, they would still not survive. The destruction that Ezekiel depicts grows now beyond its previous bounds to include more territory, and this increases the terror as well.

Ezekiel's statements about the destruction of the outlying rural areas do not reflect the Babylonian policy of leaving the surrounding countryside mostly intact. Relatively few of these people died by the sword. However, this prophecy of Ezekiel focuses on the local shrines, and the army may well have focused on the priests of these shrines much more than on the farmers and others. The Babylonians considered the priests as part of the local leadership, whom they must remove in order to make the territory safe for Babylonian occupation. Ezekiel explains this from a different viewpoint, and argues that God desires the destruction of the shrines and the people associated with them because they had violated God's law through the worship of idols.

A refrain begins in this section: "You shall know that I am Yahweh" (6:7, 10). These are the first two occurrences of this phrase in Ezekiel; it appears a total of sixty times in the book, out of seventy-four times in all the Old Testament. This distinctive phrase reveals much about Ezekiel's understanding of prophecy. A prophet speaks so that the people know who God is. Prophecy proves God, not in the sense that it logically proves that God exists or that God is powerful or all-knowing. Instead, prophecy describes the nature of God.

In Ezekiel 6, the prophet makes several statements about God's nature, and he underlines two of these assertions with the phrase, "You shall know that I am Yahweh." In the first one, the phrase concludes a statement that God will punish those who worshiped idols and other gods (6:7). Then, the people will know that Yahweh is a God who takes worship with utmost seriousness. The people must direct their worship to Yahweh, and not to any others, despite the whims of the age. In the other occurrence of this formula, Yahweh says more: "They shall know that I am Yahweh; it is not in vain that I have said I would do this *ra'* to them" (6:10). The Hebrew word *ra'* can be translated in many ways. The RSV translates it as "evil," but the NRSV renders it "disaster," and both can be right. But this is the very thing that we should know about God: Yahweh is the type of God who will not hesitate to bring evil or disaster to the people.

This is quite a harsh statement. Perhaps it is meant to convince people that the one God, Yahweh, is behind all that happens in life. There are not "good" gods that do good for people and "bad" gods that bring evil upon humans; there is only one God, Yahweh, who brings all things into being. But beyond this statement of faith, Ezekiel insists on something more. Once again, our God proves to be quite unpredictable. Though one expects good from God, evil and disaster can also come. God makes the choices and brings to humanity benefit and disaster. Relationship with this God is a risky thing, then, because it can turn out poorly, as it has for these Israelites living near Jerusalem.

Have Bags, Will Travel (12:1–16)

One sign-act from later in the book carries much the same purpose as the earlier prophecies. In Ezekiel 12, God commands the prophet to pack his bags and leave. Of course, Ezekiel does not go anywhere, since he is already in exile and there is nowhere to go, but this play-acted hasty departure makes the people think about what would be happening in Jerusalem. Ezekiel digs his way through a wall to escape in secrecy. Then God offers an explanation, which is somewhat rare for sign-acts. Ezekiel is like the prince of Jerusalem, the last remnant of the royal family still to live in Judah. This prince will try to sneak out of Jerusalem in disguise, with all his life's belongings in his bags. But Yahweh will not let this one go. The Babylonians will capture the prince, and bring him into exile with the other captives. Others in his entourage will die by the sword, but the prince will live and die in exile.

Speaking Without Words

For today's people of faith, the clear question reflects the changing world. When everything has changed and our dearest values fall to history's wayside, what do we do? When words are no longer enough, how do we speak forth God's claims?

Speaking the Unspeakable

In the face of the unspeakable, what do we say to the world? Ezekiel said little, but he *lived* in a different way. Very few of his sign-acts contain any words for him to say to the people, and in very few of them does God explain in clear terms what the signs mean. Speech is not the primary means for communication for Ezekiel's prophecy. Instead, action becomes the channel for the word of God. As action continues over years, it becomes lifestyle. Certainly, Ezekiel's prophetic sign-act requiring him to lie on his side for more than fourteen months is a very significant change of lifestyle!

Actions and lifestyles seem the most sensible way to give voice to the unspeakable. In so doing, Ezekiel communicated the essence of a God who was hard to hear over the din of the world's changes. Because the people could see the evidence of Ezekiel's relationship with God on a daily basis in the very manner of his living, they could not miss the impact of his message.

The Loudest Message

But the message comes through loud and clear: we should do the acting, and let others see and do the talking. For Ezekiel, this meant to live as God's people in the exile, to lead lives that counter the prevailing (Babylonian) culture. For us, the meaning is not much different. Much of life in our modern culture goes against our faith; a life that is distinct and separate often makes that point better than all of our words ever could. Of course, the message of actions speaks loudest when accompanied by words, even if it is only a few words, as was the case with Ezekiel. Because of his words, no one could escape his point; because of his life and actions, no one could escape the force of his message. He took great risks to live a life that was not only different, but was actually at odds with the everyday lives of common people, but his sign-acts presented his values in plain sight for all to see.

4

Making Allegories

(Ezekiel 15—17)

Ezekiel often prophesied in sign-acts, performing strange deeds that communicated his message in actions instead of words. But this prophet used more than one means of making his point. He frequently spoke, as well. Ezekiel used most of the same forms of speech that the other prophets, such as Isaiah and Jere-miah, used. It should come as no surprise, however, to discover that Ezekiel also spoke in some different ways. He described himself as a "maker of allegories" (20:49), as a teller of strange (and tall) tales. It could be said that he rarely gave a straight answer; he talked around the matter with unusual images and unorthodox analogies.[1] Israel was wood, a child, a bird (Ezekiel 15—17).

---

[1] Metaphors are figures of speech that compare a more familiar object with a less familiar one, in order to communicate insight about the relatively unknown reality. Allegories are literary devices in which each significant element of the story represents some other reality. Thus, the two are separate but closely connected and often overlapping literary features.

Of course, Ezekiel's language here is not literal. Israel was truly a nation, a group of people, but he discussed this nation in metaphorical terms. His thoughts ranged far and wide as he sought common, everyday images to which he could compare Israel and the exiles. Ezekiel knew how difficult it is to express the deepest realities in plain language. So often a speaker needs metaphors to communicate a message that hardly fits into language at all. Ezekiel's message of God was so far outside the realm of the people's experience that language came close to failing altogether, and so he created metaphors and allegories that stretched the bounds of thought. These stories go beyond the credible to talk of deep truth. More than that, these stories work to form identity. Who were Ezekiel's listeners as people of faith? They were wood, they were a woman, they were an eagle. No technical terms of theology appear in this discussion; Ezekiel doesn't bother with them. The deepest thoughts were too strange to tell in straightforward language, but in these metaphors Ezekiel crafts a language that is far too simple, and through the power of metaphor, the simple outperforms the complex.

The Language of Faith

When Ezekiel moves into metaphorical language, he does so for good reason. There is always a problem with putting faith into words. Literal language may start the process of describing faith, but it rarely seems to say enough. There's always something more waiting to be said, yearning to express itself. There's something about faith that won't fit into tight, logical propositions about the nature and function of God. That language is too cold.

In our scientific age, this presents quite a problem. Most modern people are accustomed to physical, scientific descriptions of almost everything in life. Each problem possesses its own vocabulary, from automotive mechanics to health care, from psychology to electricity. Within the system, there is a separate set of words and technical terms that correspond to everything one needs to know. If one knows the right words, then one can solve almost any problem. Terminology is tantamount to mastery.

But where are the words to describe faith? Are these faith words scientific words? For centuries, the church has said that the sciences and academics cannot understand the depths of faith. Instead, the church has developed its own language, another set of technical terms rarely heard outside church buildings. Some of these are architectural terms, such as sanctuary, chapel, chancel, apse, nave, and narthex. Once you can find your way around the building, the names for people are also peculiar to church life: clergy, laity, minister, pastor, elder, deacon, presbyter, priest, lector, and cantor. Then come the theological terms: liturgy, worship, communion, eucharist, mass, sanctification, justification, theology, Christology, ecclesiology, pneumatology, atonement, prayer, creed—and the list keeps growing and growing. Without the knowledge of terms, it seems, the church can hardly talk about its own faith.

Two problems run rampant when any religious group becomes too dependent on technical terms. First, it becomes nearly impossible to communicate the faith with anyone who doesn't already have the faith and know the words. It's a vicious circle; people must know the words in order to have faith, and the only place to learn the words is in church, but in church they use words that most people can't understand. Second, when all human thinking about God occurs in technical terms, then it is very difficult to think anything new, simply because there aren't yet any words for any new thoughts. Even if new thoughts appear, great difficulty arises when trying to share these ideas and to teach them to others. The old ways and the old words combine to form an almost unbreachable wall to progress.

Ezekiel uses simple stories about everyday events in order to break through this wall of opposition to new ideas. Though he uses simple words, he twists the stories into strikingly new and disturbing combinations. His new ideas are not pleasant ones; they shake the foundations of what the people want to believe and confront them with the new and unexpected truth of God. Ezekiel's simple stories are allegories, which are detailed symbolic devices that observe a real-life situation and offer a literary interpretation. As a maker of allegories, the prophet Ezekiel offers social critique, commenting in indirect ways upon the conditions he views around him. But he is also a theologian, examining his culture and the other exiles in terms of God's nature, and finding new, imaginative ways to explain to the people what that divine nature is and how they should respond.

You Are the Vine (15:1–8)

Agricultural life offers fertile ground for metaphors, allegories, and all varieties of figurative language that can crop up in speech. This was as true for Jesus' sayings and parables as for Ezekiel's allegories. Jesus compared God's rule to a mustard seed (Matthew 13:31–32), Jerusalem to an olive tree (Luke 13:6–9), and himself to a vine (John 15:1–6). In Jesus' use of the vine imagery, he is the vine, and his followers are the branches, who are rooted in the vine and who draw their life and their function from the vine. According to the Gospel of John, the vine is a positive image of life with God, and the vine itself represents Christ, who sustains the life of the church. But long before the Gospels, Ezekiel had used the image of the vine in a very different way.

The prophet compares the vine with the trees of the forest. Trees produce wood, a precious commodity in ancient Israel. Vines, on the other hand, do not produce much of anything. If used whole, vines were not nearly as useful as timber, which could be used for construction or other tasks. Firewood was quite valuable, but vines didn't even burn well. As Ezekiel says, "Look—when it was whole, it was not used for work, and even when fire consumes it and it burns, it still cannot be used for anything!" (15:5). Vines are worthless objects, good only to burn and then forget.

Yahweh explains that Jerusalem is just the same, and so Jerusalem will burn, and then God will forget the city. Again,

Ezekiel envisions the Babylonian army's siege of Jerusalem, which results in destruction followed by a burning that removes all trace of life and hope of possibility. All the world, like Yahweh, then forgets Jerusalem and abandons the city forever.

A Woman Named Jerusalem (16:1–63)

Ezekiel's next allegory is much longer and more complex (Ezekiel 16). It follows the life of a fictional woman who represents Jerusalem. The prophet tells the story of this woman's life from childhood, to her love affair with Yahweh, to her unfaithfulness, punishment, and restoration.

A word of caution should accompany this allegory. It is explicit material, and much of it is painful to hear. Furthermore, it is far too easy to read this story as the male god *vs.* the sinful woman. The reader must always take great pains to remember that this is an allegory; the language is never meant to be taken literally. Thus, this passage does not intend to tell us that Yahweh is male or that women are sinful and deserve punishment.

When we remember this with the necessary sensitivity, two things should be uppermost in our minds. First, allegories such as this are comparisons. The author compares what the audience does not know to what they do know, in order to teach about the unknown. Ezekiel's original audience did not know how Yahweh felt about them, and so Ezekiel compares it metaphorically to something they do know—how men accuse and abuse their wives. In no sense does this comparison intend to approve of such behavior; in fact, Ezekiel's images in other chapters are also shocking, and it seems that Ezekiel's tendency was to choose shocking, disturbing images that would make people flinch. If his audience could listen to this allegory with impunity, with cold uninvolved insensitivity, I think that Ezekiel would have been quite disappointed in them. Second, we modern readers must realize how subtly powerful these images are to us. Our own culture condones the abuse of women to such a high degree that it is almost impossible for most modern readers to have escaped this influence. If Ezekiel's allegories do not thoroughly shock us, then we have not only missed the prophet's point, but we have succumbed to the faithlessness of our generation, to an extent that is surely more than we care to admit to ourselves.

Birth (16:1–7)

The story begins in a way that is far from innocent, but that only distantly foreshadows the horrors to come. Jerusalem is born, and Yahweh judges that by birth this child is a Canaanite. For the ancient Jewish reader, this would have been quite an insult, on religious grounds, but one that they would grudgingly confess as accurate. Though Israel felt that they had grown far beyond their Canaanite roots, that was their undeniable past. Israel's birth was an unpleasant affair. Israel began in Egypt, as slaves who barely escaped with their lives and who wandered in a desert on the brinks of death for a full generation, before they acquired a tentative toehold in a new land. Ezekiel likens their origins to a baby girl abandoned at birth, without the basic care that a newborn requires.[2] But Yahweh passes by, and sees the child whose death was only hours away, and God utters hardly more than a word: "Live." The child lives and grows.

Love (16:8–14)

The second scene of this lengthy allegory is somewhat more pleasant. Yahweh once again passes by the child Jerusalem, who has now passed through adolescence alone, without family or anyone to care for her. This time, Yahweh offers more than a word; God stops and pays attention to her. This

---

[2] In the ancient world, fathers often valued sons much more than daughters, and a common practice called "exposure" killed unwanted newborn daughters by placing them outside the range of hearing, where they would die by starvation or by animals over the course of hours or days. It is sadly striking that Yahweh here does not condemn that practice, but merely counteracts it in one exceptional (and fictional) instance.

waif has become an attractive, sexy young woman, and she catches Yahweh's eye. Sex and marriage soon follow, and Yahweh dotes over her, providing all the material goods of life, especially jewelry and other adornments to enhance her appearance. Yahweh transforms her into the beauty queen, as if God were a man who would be proud to have such a woman on his arm. Together as husband and wife, they cut a dashing figure through international society, and Yahweh gladly takes all the credit for her attractiveness.

But already are sown the hints of discord. Yahweh and Jerusalem have a very superficial relationship. After leaving her alone for years, Yahweh steps in and notices only her appearance, and even that works to God's benefit more than Jerusalem's. There is no language of a mutual relationship of love. In the absence of commitment and the overwhelming presence of appearance and physical attraction, the destruction of the relationship seems imminent.

Unfaithfulness (16:15–34)

The very next verse reverses the story from its idyllic picture of beauty and love to a nightmare of condemnation. God accuses Jerusalem of horrible things. She trusted in her appearance, and that reliance began her downfall. Then, the accusations grow. She became unfaithful to her husband, Yahweh, having sex with any passing stranger. She took the gifts that Yahweh had given her and she used them to make idols, which she then worshiped. She sacrificed her own sons and daughters, the children of God, to false deities. She did all this with no comprehension of the depths from which Yahweh had raised her (16:22).[3]

---

[3] Surely, this is the intention of Ezekiel 16:22, to argue that Jerusalem should have considered the things that Yahweh had done for her. But the argument loses its coherence when it reminds Jerusalem of how she was when was born. The problem is that Yahweh had neglected her in the days of her youth, taking notice of her only once she was grown. Ezekiel 16:22 commands Jerusalem to consider the days in which Yahweh abandoned her. Perhaps this implies a threat.

The catalog of accusations reaches a frenzy, climaxing with descriptions of Jerusalem's enticing of other nations. First mentioned are the Egyptians, Jerusalem's southern neighbors; Yahweh claims that Jerusalem consorted with Egypt for the sole purpose of provoking Yahweh's wrath. Next come the Philistines, who were ashamed of the extent of Jerusalem's abandon, thus they exacted retribution in ways that Yahweh finds justified. Then Yahweh accuses Jerusalem of intimacy with Assyria, because Jerusalem had still wanted more lovers; Babylonia, too, joins the list of adulterers. Finally, Yahweh demeans Jerusalem as worse than a common prostitute; whereas prostitutes charge fees for their services, Jerusalem gave money to strangers to bribe them into sex.[4] In this way, none of Jerusalem's consorts were worthy of blame for their misdeeds; Jerusalem alone was entirely at fault—or so the story goes.

Punishment (16:35–52)

Yahweh ceases to list accusations; God's role as prosecutor gives way to a new role as judge. Yahweh now passes sentence on Jerusalem, declaring her severe punishment. First, Yahweh will gather all of her co-adulterers from throughout the world into one place, and in their presence Yahweh will strip the clothes from Jerusalem and display her nakedness (16:37).[5] Then, Jerusalem's lovers will destroy all of her buildings and belongings. Next, they will stone her and slice her with the sword. After Yahweh burns her and her property to the ground, then will God's wrath be satisfied (16:42–43). Once this destruction is complete, then Yahweh will once more blame Jerusalem for these things, claiming that immorality ran in her family and that she was the worst of the lot. Even after the punishment, Jerusalem still receives the blame; she only deserves the violence done against her.

---

[4] Does this compare the "woman" Jerusalem to the more depraved (stereotypically, men) who purchase sex from others?

[5] This phrase, "uncovering her nakedness," may refer to public rape (cp. Jeremiah 13:22; Genesis 9:20–24), but this is uncertain.

Restoration (16:53–63)

The restoration that comes at the end of the allegory does not apply to Jerusalem at all. Instead, all of Jerusalem's enemies will be restored, so that they can laugh at her and increase her shame. God will fully restore Samaria, the evil capital of the northern kingdom of Israel, but will not restore Jerusalem. Likewise, nations all around Judah will be strengthened and revived. God will even return Sodom to its glorious days of old, but will leave Jerusalem as a shameful desolation.

At the end, however, Jerusalem receives a new covenant with God (16:62). It is not at all clear what that covenant contains, but it may set forth a new basis for a relationship between Yahweh and Jerusalem. Still, the purpose of the covenant is clear: even after Yahweh forgives Jerusalem, the city must still live in shame and desecration because of its sins. There is no true salvation for Jerusalem in this allegory, only an endless continuation of its agony.

The political equivalents of this long and painful allegory seem evident. Yahweh condemns Jerusalem for its consistent seeking of advantage through international alliances. Because of Judah's alliances with Assyria, Egypt, and Babylonia, these nations (if not others) will destroy Jerusalem and will not allow it to be rebuilt. Ezekiel uses the most shocking, violent language to depict this political reality. International intrigue causes the city's devastation, and Ezekiel compares it to Yahweh as a violent wife-beater, claiming in a hollow voice that it is her fault. Yahweh's raging anger grows out of proportion to the wrongs attributed to Jerusalem, and perhaps this represents the most disturbing aspect of this allegory. In Ezekiel 16, God shows no mercy, but punishes to death in the heat of anger and jealousy. God is a disruptive, destructive deity who gives no thought to appropriate limits or respect of others. This vision of God is most sobering, most distressing.

Eagles' Wings (17:1–21)

Ezekiel's next allegory derives its images from birds. The prophet tells the story of two large eagles. The first eagle visits trees and plants and chooses twigs and seeds to plant in a new land. These sprout and take hold, and produce good foliage. In this new land, the seeds grow and the vine prospers. But then the new vine spots another magnificent, beautiful eagle in the sky, and it longs to be with the second eagle. The vine signals into the sky, attracting the new eagle's attention, and soon this eagle swoops out of the sky and plucks up the growing vine, taking it through the sky to transplant it in another faraway place. But God has a question: will the vine prosper now? The answer is that the vine cannot regain its strength once the second eagle transplants it; the vine will wither and die in its new home.

This allegory is more difficult to understand; its point is certainly subtler than Ezekiel's previous tale of Yahweh and the wife Jerusalem. Fortunately, Ezekiel explains the story of the eagles and the vine in the political terms that he intends as the relevant comparison (17:11–21). The vine symbolizes the king of Jerusalem, whom the Babylonian army took away into exile, just as a majestic eagle swoops down and takes away its prey. This allows the royal family, the vine, to prosper; life in exile is not necessarily a bad thing.

But then the vine grows restless and looks for another eagle. There was a new king in Jerusalem who attempted some political intrigue by searching for another ally that might restore Jerusalem as a separate kingdom. This king thought that he had found such an ally in Egypt, but Babylonia had already replanted the vine in exile, and the vine could not survive another transplantation. The political message thus unfolds: the Judean royal family should not campaign for Egypt's favor. The royalty who were in exile could prosper in Babylonia, but any of royal family left in Jerusalem who allied themselves with Egypt would surely wither away. A king in Jerusalem who rebelled against Babylonian rule would be promptly taken into exile, and there he would die. Instead, those in exile should consider themselves fortunate, because they had received the possibility of life and prosperity. God favors and chooses life in Babylonia, even though that land is evil.

Violence and Destruction All Around

These allegories, disturbing as they are, combine in one direction. Ezekiel wishes the people to know deeply that there is no possibility of life in Jerusalem. Only life in exile can be part of God's intention; the exiles should abandon any plans or notions of return. Ezekiel's images of the useless vine (chapter 15) and the transplanted vine that withers (chapter 17) are harsh portrayals of the possibilities of life in Jerusalem; the allegory of Jerusalem as Yahweh's punished and humiliated wife (chapter 16) is even more distressing. It is not enough for Ezekiel to assert that Babylonia is the right place for the Jews to live; the prophet goes far beyond to show the utter degradation of life anywhere else. Anywhere near Jerusalem there is violence and destruction; terror is all around.[6]

Ezekiel works hard to extinguish any and all hope of returning to Jerusalem. These Jews in exile must stay there! They must accept their lot in life as an assignment from God. Any other course of action would meet with swift retribution. Moreover, the people *deserve* their diminished life as Babylonian exiles. If this life is an existence of dire suffering, then so be it. The people have earned such punishment through their consistent, vile sinning. Exile is appropriate for such depraved persons; they should not seek any better life.[7]

Yet a brief note of hope enters into Ezekiel's prophecy right after these stark, depressing allegorical messages. Someday Yahweh will take a twig and plant it in Israel, and this new twig will grow and flourish. Then all the trees and nations of the world will know that Yahweh is God. Yahweh's nature is to raise up the humble and humiliated peoples of the world and to oppress the proud ones (17:22–24). After Israel receives the full measure of its punishment, then there will be a chance for restoration. But this will happen someday, possibly in the very

---

[6] There are striking similarities to the starkness and anguish of Jeremiah 20, though the situation is much different.

[7] However, life in Babylonia is not necessarily a *bad* life, as it would be in other biblical books, such as Revelation.

distant future, and certainly there can be no restoration until Israel has fallen to the deepest of the depths.

It almost seems too much to hope for any kind of restoration after Ezekiel's earlier rejection of any positive messages. Many scholars have suggested that 17:22–24 is an addition to the book by an editor well after Ezekiel's time, who could not bear the sustained negativity of the prophet. This note of hope may also represent a later point within Ezekiel's own ministry, when he would update this early saying to show the possibilities for hope that had grown into being through the course of the exiles' life. But it seems likely that this final, hopeful note is not too distant from the allegories of Ezekiel 15—17. In the allegories, there is a consistent hope for the exiles who live in Babylonia, and in 17:22–24, that hope remains: life is possible in Babylonia, but someday maybe you can go back after God's wrath upon Jerusalem is fully vented. For the time being, though, it's best to stay in exile. God is a God of reversals, making the high into the low and vice versa. On the other hand, there is never any hope for the inhabitants of Jerusalem. In the allegories, God and Babylonia destroy the Jerusalemites, and in 17:22–24 God replaces anyone left in the city with new inhabitants. There is hope, but it is only hope for those ready to live for a generation or more in Babylonian exile. God has placed them in that strange, foreign land, and there they must stay and prosper—or else.

Making Allegories

In order to communicate these strange and intense messages, Ezekiel chooses to employ allegories. Ezekiel's use of allegories points out two things for religious persons of all ages, including ours. The first is that the church must choose strange, striking images for the expression of its theology and the telling of its own story. A world such as ours hears best when we tell our story in surprising ways. Certainly, this was true for Ezekiel and his world; his words were quite memorable and have succeeded in surviving for over two and a half millennia, in no small part because they were so striking and unfamiliar from their very beginning. The fantastic and the unbelievable are also the most noticeable and the most memorable.[8]

Second, the church must use common language. Ezekiel does not use technical terms of theology, but instead phrases his convictions in common language. Though his ideas are strange, anyone can understand them, because the language is that of the family, of the farm, of the animals. He says things that the uneducated can understand and that the non-religious can believe. These should be our goals, too. When we use this common language, avoiding the technical terms, it becomes more possible for us to think new thoughts and to realize new things about God. Even if we hold fast to the notion that God doesn't change, our understandings of God must keep growing, and thus we keep needing new ideas, and common language serves us best in forming these new thoughts about God, just as was the case for Ezekiel so long ago.

---

[8] Ezekiel goes beyond the surprising to be perverse and offensive. Even though these techniques are memorable and, in some ways, effective, it does not mean that we today should be equally offensive. Each word and story carries multiple layers of meaning and effects, and should always be used with care.

5

Morality and Responsibility

(Ezekiel 18)

The allegories of the previous chapter end with a tenuous note of hope. Someday, there will be a restoration of the people, and in that day the Babylonian exiles will return to Jerusalem and start their lives over again. This restoration in the indefinite, distant future offers some possibility for hope in the exile's present, though it is clear that their current suffering will continue for the immediate future. Ezekiel 18 maintains this note of hope and develops it in a new direction. This chapter discusses ethics and asserts how the people should live, both in the present troubles and in the day to come when restoration brings them new life.

Fate, Freedom, and Responsibility

Ezekiel 18 deals with the problem of individual responsibility. Will God truly hold each person accountable for each's own actions? This approach emphasizes morality not only as things to be done and things to be avoided, but as a sense that one's own deeds really matter. Thus, this sense of responsibility may be considered as the opposite of the notion of fate. If fate rules the universe, then it does not matter what any one person does. The results of life are inevitable, unchangeable, and completely unrelated to what someone does. If bad things happen, blame someone else. If good things happen, be thankful but don't think that you made them happen. In our society, fate often ties into freedom. Because the results are determined anyway, I can do whatever I want, and it won't matter. I can't change anything; I'm just one person in a big world. Too often, our notions of freedom focus on action without consequence, instead of on tough decision making and the willingness to accept the consequences. But Ezekiel insists on ultimate individual responsibility. Everything we do matters, and we must face the consequences.

Now, in God's new way of living with the people, each person is responsible for that one's own actions. No longer are we held responsible for the sins of the previous generation. This brings a great deal of hope to a people who live in exile, because they can see that they can rise out of their problems. Responsibility means the potential for rising above the difficulties of life, though it also carries a great burden because of the urgent need for moral action. For Ezekiel, responsibility also means that the people deserve what has befallen them. Their evil actions have received their just rewards, and this has meant divine punishment. This radical emphasis on responsibility can become a demanding, demeaning aspect of faith, but in Ezekiel's development of it here are the glimmers of hope for a suffering people who desire a new life.

A Proverb (18:1–4)

Ezekiel and Jeremiah both discuss a catchy proverb: "The parents eat unripe grapes, and the children's teeth grate"

(Jeremiah 31:29–30; Ezekiel 18:2).[1] Presumably, this was a familiar proverb to people in those days. Unripe, sour fruit has a grating effect on the teeth, and this proverb turns this fact into a statement of the connection between generations. When one generation participates in an activity, the results of that activity fall upon the next generation. Modern American English contains similar proverbs, such as "like father, like son." But our proverbs tend to focus on similarities in nature; parents and children tend to share a common character. This ancient Hebrew proverb emphasizes the effects of actions between the generations. Each generation's activities affect the experiences of the next generation. In our own day, this insight into human existence has given rise to sayings about ecology, such as, "We do not inherit the earth from our parents; we borrow it from our children."[2]

In Ezekiel's time, the popular proverb about grapes might have operated to explain their current situation. Why is our generation suffering? It is because our parents broke God's will and did disastrous deeds; now we pay the punishment for what they did. The psychological impact of such thinking is immense. People can say, "It's not my fault—it's their fault," "I didn't have anything to do with it," and more depressing things such as, "What could I do about it? These things just happen to me and there's no way to stop it." Such thinking verges on the loss of hope. When people do not feel in control of their events, they lose the reason to change their own environments. People who see themselves as out of control and

---

[1] With one change, I follow the translation of Gordon H. Matties, *Ezekiel 18 and the Rhetoric of Moral Discourse* (SBL Dissertation Series 126; Atlanta: Scholars Press, 1990). This book contains many valuable insights into Ezekiel 18's function in creating a ground for a new community.

[2] Our own generation can profit immensely from such proverbs, especially around topics such as the ecology and federal budget deficits. The church must deal with crises such as these, and be aware of its own involvement in shaping the options for the next generation. We need to recognize our own responsibility as a community for affecting the world of tomorrow. But such is not precisely Ezekiel's point here.

hopeless may not realize what they can do to improve their situation or to make moral choices.

For these reasons, Ezekiel rejects this proverb. He works against the hopelessness that exile could engender, desiring that the people work together to form a new moral community. Thus, Yahweh offers a corrective to the proverb: it is the one who sins who will suffer the consequences of that act (18:4). No one else pays the price for one's sin; God will punish only the sinner. This provides a word of hope, because in this new era of responsibility, it is possible to control the events of one's own life. If one wishes to live without punishment, then all one must do is avoid sin. Of course, there are still things in life beyond individual control; Ezekiel does not suggest that the exiles return to their land and start their nation over again. The exile is an unavoidable fact, but it need not be a continuing punishment for those who have not sinned. Indeed, exile can be the place of life with God, if the people will keep themselves free from sin.

A New Morality (18:5–13)

By reversing the proverb of the grapes and the teeth, Ezekiel provides a motivation for morality. One's own actions affect one's own life, and so ethical actions are important. Next, Ezekiel moves to a description of the morality that God requires. The prophet provides a list of right and wrong behavior:

If one is righteous and does what is lawful and right—
if one does not eat upon the mountains,
if one does not lift up the eyes to the idols of the house of Israel,
if one does not violate a neighbor's marriage,
if one does not approach another for illicit sexual behavior,
if one does not oppress anyone and restores the pledge to a debtor,

if one does not commit robbery, but gives bread to the
   hungry and covers the naked with a garment,
if one does not accept advance interest,
if one does not take accrued interest,
but if one withholds the hand from iniquity,
if one does truth and justice between people,
if one follows my statutes,
if one keeps my judgments to perform truth—
such a one is righteous;
such a one shall surely live,
says the Lord Yahweh.

Ezekiel 18:5–9

At first glance, there seems no order to this list, but the
various elements of the moral life presented here fall into two
general categories: correct worship and social compassion. The
commitment to justice and social compassion shines clearly
through this list. People should not take advantage of others,
avoiding the opportunities to take undue profit at others'
expense. Instead, people should realize that, in our small world,
it is beneficial to watch after the benefits of others, giving
generously of food and clothing when those needs arise. This
kind of realization, resulting in deep individual commitment
to caring for each other, can provide the foundation for a new
order of society. In this vision, people live together in harmony, sharing the prosperity that God gives and protecting the
interests of each other. This allows social stability and true
peace.

But morality is more than taking the proper care of each
other, as important as that is. According to Ezekiel, worship is
also a necessary moral act. It is interesting to watch what
Ezekiel includes and what he omits. Ezekiel excludes all mention of belief, such as the things we typically call faith. The
prophet is very interested in proper worship, but does not deal
with theology or belief. It is not so much the belief in certain
statements about God that makes one moral, in his thinking;
the morality comes from the worship together with the com-

munity. Of course, worship itself is strongly theological, since
it is an enactment of belief. But the particular statements and
creeds of faith are missing from Ezekiel's list.[3] The emphasis
falls upon the worshiping community and the togetherness
forged in common worship. Thus, Ezekiel's morality connects
most strongly to the communal sense of the people as one
group in service of God.

Thus, the required worship complements the necessary
social concern. Both serve to strengthen the sense of community that appears as the true goal of morality. To violate the
community is to violate morality; to live the moral life means to
feel and work for the benefit of the community. In this vision of
a new morality, Ezekiel offers a renewed and energized option
for life in community. Within this type of world, restoration
would not only be possible, but would become inevitable.

The restoration of society into this newly vibrant community becomes a possibility because of individual responsibility.
When people are each responsible to care for each other, and
when individual moral action is indeed possible, then this
community can attain its promise. The restoration of society,
then, begins on a very personal level, but it soon expands into
responsibility for the whole of the community. That is the
exiles' hope for restoration.[4]

The Next Generation (18:14–20)

Before the hope grows too quickly in his audience's mind,
Ezekiel inserts a note of caution. Individual responsibility does
not give to the current generation a permanent ability to solve
the community's problems. When the next generation comes,
they too will have to make their choices and live with the
results of their actions. "The righteous one's righteousness will

---

[3] This point can be seen clearly by comparing Ezekiel 18 with other
similar lists, such as the Ten Commandments (Exodus 20; Deuteronomy
5), which begins with creedal statements about God's nature and activity.

[4] For another discussion of this important passage, see Jon L. Berquist,
*Ancient Wine, New Wineskins: The Lord's Supper in Old Testament Perspec-
tive* (St. Louis, Missouri: Chalice Press, 1991), chapter 7.

be upon the righteous one; the wicked one's wickedness will be upon the wicked one" (18:20). Thus, it is possible for the community to heal itself, but the choices will always reside before the people, in each generation. Ezekiel asserts that true changes are possible; unfortunately, that also means that there can be bad changes, as well.

Because of this, any restoration may not be a permanent one. No generation has the ability or the right to make choices for the next. What remains in the background of this passage in Ezekiel is the importance of education. It is not enough to pass down to the next generation the established customs and institutions, or to teach them the right answers. Education involves training each generation, by example and also by word, to think morally. They will face new situations, when all the moral action of their parents will not solve their new problems. They must then be able to make the difficult decisions for themselves, in order for the restoration of society to continue apace through the years.

Of course, the need for such education crosses more boundaries than the generational one. Ezekiel's emphasis on individual responsibility means that morality and communal restoration are only as strong as the weakest link. Education is required to enable all persons to participate in the moral community. It is never enough to provide answers to others, to legislate the right action. True morality comes not from the actions or from the beliefs, but from the dedication to the community and from the active decision making of individuals to uphold that community. Such is true morality, and teaching moral thinking becomes the task for all persons, for every age, just as the responsibility for morality itself devolves upon every person. The need for each one's commitment to morality is greater than any of us imagine.

God's Pleasure, God's Pain (18:21–24)

As Ezekiel explains the situation, God allows for individual responsibility, and this provides the possibility for moral action that forms a restored community. On the other hand, God will not prevent the human choices that destroy the community and the opportunities for restoration. All options are open; humans must choose between good and evil, and God will require that they live with their own consequences.

But it should not be thought that Yahweh is impartial, as if God was a dispassionate judge who sat at the sidelines and calmly observed the affairs of humanity without any emotional reactions at all. To the contrary, God is intimately involved with human decisions and with the lives that humans create for themselves. God's interest is not in punishing or in settling the score. God has an intense bias in the whole process of human decision making. God desires repentance with a fierce, burning, overwhelming desire. Yahweh takes pleasure when people choose the ways that lead to life and to restoration.

In this passage resounds a faint echo of Deuteronomy 30:15–20. At the end of a long sermon, Moses offers a conclusion: "I call heaven and earth as witnesses to you this day. I have set before you life and death, blessing and cursing. Therefore, choose life, so that you and your descendants may live" (Deuteronomy 30:19). Moses' words, like Yahweh's thoughts in Ezekiel 18, are far from impartial. Moses presents the choices clearly and sets them before the people, realizing that they will make their own choices and thus determine their own future, but he desires that they make the choices that will lead to life. In the same fashion, God's pleasure lies in human moral decisions that reflect the right attitudes toward morality and community.

God's pleasure in human morality points interestingly at a parallel that remains undiscussed. If God feels and expresses delight at people's right choices, does God feel pain when humans make mistakes? The tenor of the passage suggests that there is a divine hurting at the follies of humanity. If this is the case, then there is an additional insight into God's nature. Yahweh feels with the people; our human choices not only determine our own futures but motivate God's emotions. Certainly, God is not passive in Ezekiel 18, but perhaps we can say more than that. God's compassion drives Yahweh to feel with humans and for humans, and here we gain the most profound insight into God's reasons for seeking our life.

Toward a Doctrine of Fairness (18:25–29)

This next section of Ezekiel's discussion on morality cautions us about a potent and dangerous trap: blaming God for the problems that we face. Yahweh indignantly wonders why people would say that God is not fair, and then returns the question to the people. Why are the exiles not fair and just in their dealings? Why are they not willing to play fair with God, joining God in the project of bringing morality to the world? Both God and the people accuse each other of failing to contribute enough to their joint efforts of building the community. Better phrased, the people fail to recognize God's contributions. They sense only their own suffering, and never notice that God hurts with them. Blinded to the divine compassion, the exiles misunderstand and disrespect God's involvement with them.

The point is much more than the respect of God, however. The people must be willing to contribute what God requires. Whining and quibbling offer no substitutes for the real work of building the moral community. Once again, God encourages the people to take responsibility for their actions; this is the key to this passage, as well as the previous ones. God is utterly serious in the divine insistence on human individual responsibility, and will allow no disagreement. Whether humans consider this fair is immaterial; God will enforce responsibility.

A New Heart (18:30–32)

The passage ends with another note of hope. God cries out to the people: "Make for yourselves a new heart and a new spirit!" (18:31). Completely new possibilities reside just within reach for these exiles. They possess the amazing ability to transcend their sin and their suffering and to begin a new life with God, a life in responsible faithfulness and in moral community. Their suffering is quite serious; they can deal with it only through a complete repudiation of their former selves and the construction of a new existence. But this new heart and new spirit are available for them; they are realistic options for their immediate future. There is reason to hope in the future, because through their own responsibility the people have the ability to change themselves, to restore their community, and to live lives that are thoroughly worthwhile.

This note of hope, however, is not without an overtone of challenge. The change set before them is a massive alteration of their entire lives. It is not a cosmetic change; it is a deep rethinking of their reasons to live. It is an inner transformation of unparalleled dimensions. Everything hangs in the balance, precariously dependent upon their own willingness to start life with God anew. Utter commitment will suffice, and nothing less. New hearts await, but the old ones must first be removed, and that will doubtless be the most painful of operations. Fresh spirits can revive these ailing exiles, but they must first thoroughly exhale the dead air of their former lives. They receive the unexpected, surprising offer of a chance to start anew, to begin again in a radically new way, and new beginnings are always most frightening.

Hope and Retribution

Throughout this entire chapter of Ezekiel, hope and retribution combine themselves in surprising fashion. Restoration appears possible, enabling a hope in a future that may surpass the pain of the present. But retribution lurks in the wings of every verse, waiting to reverse our perceptions of this chapter's intent and God's role in our lives. God seems punitive at points. Even when the people cry out against God's unfairness, God turns a deaf ear to them, accusing them of unfairness and laziness in their own situations. Restoration and hope are possible if the people change so completely that there is hardly anything left that they would recognize, because God will so thoroughly destroy the people's old selves. The choice seems most starkly drawn: either the people find hope and restoration or complete destruction. No middle ground exists, and this lack bothers us. If only God would accept a halfway effort, perhaps we would stand a better chance. But God wants everything, or nothing, and the standards seem so high.

Yet there is hope that stems from God's faithfulness. In Ezekiel 16, when the prophet told the allegory of Jerusalem as God's wife, the readers saw the pain of God, lashing out in the form of destructive, abusive, unreasoning anger. The devastation and humiliation of that fictional woman Jerusalem knew no sensible bounds; we cry with the exiles that her level of responsibility could not have justified this severity of punishment. But here, Yahweh assures us that there is no pleasure in the people's death. The anger subsides, and we see clearly God's compassionate, sympathetic pain. Because God feels for us and with us, there is hope, and that hope lies chiefly in God's willingness to make new lives for us, through our participation in the moral, responsible community. God's own commitment to the process of our own change gives us reason to hope that the fullness of change is a realistic possibility.

Responsibility and Morality

At the root of this divine possibility for our new lives is a deep sense of personal, individual responsibility. Each of us *must* contribute to the cause. There are no other choices except destruction; there is no middle ground. There is no one else to blame, not our parents nor even God. We are each responsible. This leads to an absolute insistence on morality. For Ezekiel, morality means primarily two things: proper worship in the community that strives for morality, and caring for the members of the community with their own social welfare uppermost in our minds. Again, no exceptions are granted; we are *responsible*. We are responsible for living in the community that worships God, and we are responsible for doing whatever it take to ensure each other's well-being. These items are not negotiable. But when we listen carefully to the prophet Ezekiel, we do not hear commands for other actions, such as protecting the faith or adhering to any sort of orthodoxy or purging our communities of the undesirables. Such acts are not part of Ezekiel's morality. The acceptance of all others who join in the worship of God and the protection of their welfare contains all the relevant morality.

Such is a message that today's church needs to hear again. We are each held responsible for our own sin. We are glad to hear that we will not be held responsible for the past, because that means that our problems in this generation are solvable. We can do it. But there's a catch. This means that we *must* solve them. This provides the basis for a new seriousness about sin and a fresh commitment to solving the problems around us. Even the most deeply ingrained structural evil can be fought—and we must do it. We are responsible.

6

A Tale of Two Sisters

(Ezekiel 23)

Ezekiel's tendency to produce complex allegories became apparent in chapters 15—17, when the prophet told Jerusalem's story in terms of a vine, a woman, and two eagles. We saw how allegories use ordinary language in most extraordinary, surreal ways to speak new, surprising ideas about God. These allegories shock our sensibilities, as they intend to do, in order to communicate radically new thoughts. Ezekiel uses dangerous language in his allegories, and we must interpret these dangerous images with utmost caution. The images are so powerful that they nearly overwhelm the reader, and in this case they threaten unbelievable degrees of violence and pain.

Like Ezekiel's earlier allegories, the tale of two sisters tells the story of Jerusalem's destruction, a painful story that increases its agony with each retelling. The Jews who now lived in Babylonia felt that the destruction of Jerusalem had been the most devastating, degrading event in their lives, and so Ezekiel compared it to other moments of intense humiliation and anguish. When Ezekiel borrows disturbing images, such as rape, we must not think that he condones such evil practices, but only that he notices the violence surrounding him and uses such horrible images to speak about the reality of exile.

Despite his need to shock in order to inform, Ezekiel presents the reader with such a nightmarish vision that one cannot help but wonder the value of relying on such imagery. Through this allegory, we receive messages on several levels. We not only learn about the experience of exile, as seen through Ezekiel's eyes, but we also begin to perceive the theological choices confronting those who would interpret the exile. Empowered by this perception, we can sense the cost of choosing certain theological positions. Once again, we find ourselves debating, as did Ezekiel's first audience, the nature of God.[1]

The Story of the Two Sisters (23:1–4)

The story begins with two young women who were prostitutes in Egypt. Already, the tale reminds us of the allegory in Ezekiel 16, where the young woman attracted Yahweh's attention but then turned to other lovers, and readers are right to expect a similar story of excruciating pain. The stories, however, are different in many respects, and they deserve individual attention. In this tale of two sisters, Ezekiel describes them as residents of Egypt. These women become symbols of Israel's early years, when the Hebrew people still served as Pharaoh's slaves in Egypt, before God raised Moses as a redeemer to lead them out of bondage. Just as Israel became Yahweh's chosen people, these women entered into the relationship of marriage with God, who took them away from

---

[1] For another discussion of Ezekiel 23, set in the context of the Hebrew Bible's depictions about women, see Jon L. Berquist, *Reclaiming Her Story: The Witness of Women in the Old Testament* (St. Louis, Missouri: Chalice Press, 1992), chapter 10.

Egypt.[2] Thus, the story begins with echoes of salvation, reminiscent of the Exodus.

The two sisters have unique names: Oholah and Oholibah. Oholah may mean "her tent," signifying Samaria, the capital of the northern kingdom of Israel. Oholibah may mean "my tent is in her," and refers to Jerusalem.[3] The term *tent* reminds the reader of God's first dwelling place among the Israelites, in the Tent of Meeting.[4] This portable shrine sufficed for the worship of God until Solomon's construction of the Jerusalem temple. Though the exact implications of the names cannot be determined, they certainly would have triggered in the first audience's minds the old tent and the issues of worship, which the allegory later mentions explicitly.

This allegory's short introduction says much in a few words. Already we know about the sisters whom Yahweh saved from Egypt. We know that prostitution will once again be a dominant metaphor for disregarding Yahweh, and we know that north Israel and Judah will be the subject of the political discussion. With these statements, the allegory begins in earnest.

Oholah (23:5–10)

Immediately, the sisters went astray. Oholah, the older sister, led the way in her transgression. She paid too much attention to the Assyrians, and the allegory compares this to a return to her previous prostitution. Ezekiel's description of her

---

[2] The women also bore sons and daughters to Yahweh. Perhaps Ezekiel intends the women to represent the ruling classes of the cities and the children as the common folk of Israel and Judah. If so, then the commoners are blameless, though they become the innocent victims of the national government (23:10, 39). Though this interpretation is possible, the evidence in its favor is too weak to insist upon it.

[3] Quite possibly, the verse's explanation of the names' correlation to Samaria and Jerusalem was a subsequent addition for the benefit of later readers who did not know the history as well. The first readers might have understood the allegory without such assistance.

[4] See Exodus 29, 30, 40.

involvement with the enemy nation took on increasingly sinister and sexual overtones. Two of her mistakes received special attention: she depended on the warriors and she defiled herself with the idols (23:7). Samaria had been an overly political capital, concerned with attracting the military protection, and the leadership was willing to worship whatever gods might gain them international prestige and power. These were the sins of Samaria.

Yahweh punished Oholah for her transgression. God delivered her into the hands of her former lovers, the Assyrians, and they ravaged her. They raped her and kidnapped her children, and then they killed her by the sword. For her sins, she lost her life, but only after she lost her dignity and her selfhood, only after she watched her children die before her own eyes. Her loss became complete, and Yahweh, her husband, never shed a tear, as if nothing had ever happened.

Oholibah's Crime (23:11–21)

The allegory then moved to depict Oholah's sister, Oholibah, which is Jerusalem. This comparison was more pressing upon the minds of Ezekiel's exilic audience, and so the prophet spent much more time explaining her situation. Oholibah was more corrupt in every way than her sister, according to the allegory. She exceeded her older sister in every sin that Oholah had ever committed. Both Oholah and Oholibah pursued the Assyrians, and this love affair resulted in Oholah's destruction. But Oholibah took this affair one step further. While consorting with the Assyrians, Oholibah saw pictures on the wall, and she lusted after the Babylonians portrayed therein. She sent messengers to them, inviting them to share her favors. But soon she tired of the Babylonians, and sent them away in disgust, turning back to the Egyptians.

The last century of Jerusalem's politics parallels these accusations against Oholibah. Nearly one hundred fifty years before the exile, Assyria had conquered Israel to the north and had threatened to destroy Judah and Jerusalem, too. In those times Judah had repeatedly considered alliances with Assyria or with other nations in order to purchase their own security. But these repeated alliances proved dangerous because the Jerusalem politicians had great difficulty measuring the geopolitical winds. Their many mistakes threatened their very existence. One of those alliances was with Babylonia. However, Assyria soon met its end in battle against the Babylonians, and then Judah wanted no further association with them. Jerusalem instead courted Egypt, because they seemed the only power that could protect tiny Judah from the rapacious Babylonia.

Oholibah's Punishment (23:22–35)

Because Oholibah's sin exceeded that of her sister, Oholibah's punishment also grew beyond all measure. Yahweh handed the older sister over to one nation, Assyria, but God forced Oholibah to suffer indignation from several nations, with the Babylonians in the lead. The nations came against her fully armed, with the world's greatest military technology, overwhelming the impoverished Jerusalem. Not only did Oholibah suffer rape, but also mutilation and dismemberment (23:25, 34). The punishment's severity transcended even the horrendous acts against Samaria and Israel.

In the last verse of this section, Ezekiel detailed Oholibah's crucial sin. She disregarded Yahweh. Instead, Jerusalem's concerns had focused on the international politics and the necessities of survival. For small nations to endure international turmoils, they had to sell themselves to the bigger nations, who could protect them from others. That was reality in the ancient world, just as it is in the modern day. But Ezekiel insisted that Judah should have ignored the conventional wisdom and trusted only in its own God, defying the advances of the world powers. Judah's sin was trusting in military power and the prowess of its negotiators, instead of in God.[5]

---

[5] This is a common theme of the Hebrew prophets, especially in the eighth century and in the times right before the exile.

The Punishment of the Two Sisters (23:36–45)

The two sisters have already received their punishment, but God prolonged considering what should happen to them. The condemnation continued: they cared more for politics than for God. Not only their acts were evil, but their intentions and especially the energy with which they pursued their sexual liaisons with their lovers, their political alliances with other nations.

The end of this section shows a terrifying side of God. Yahweh noticed that the sisters no longer desired their sexual encounters. They had stopped their lusting, but they could not stop the advances of their partners. Now the sexual event was rape, pure and simple. When God paused to evaluate this, however, what God saw was the previous activity. Though the situation changed, God did not allow the new reality to affect the divine judgment. There would be no mercy, no adjustment of the penalty because of mitigating circumstances. There was only punishment.

Allegories represent reality from a particular perspective. From the allegory's perspective, certain elements of reality appear with crystalline clarity, but other points remain unseen. For this reason, allegories always distort the reality that they portray. All allegories leave out something, and this allegory omits any mention of the men. The sin of adultery is committed by two people, but the partners of Oholah and Oholibah received no punishment at all. Why not? Certainly the sins of Assyria and Babylonia were great, and at other points the prophets condemned these other nations with great ferocity, but in this allegory, the evil empires seemed almost blameless. The unwillingness to condemn the empires combined with the overeagerness to accuse and punish the women bespeaks the pathology of this text. Only the victims receive blame.

The Destruction (23:46–49)

The severe punishments of the previous sections proved insufficient for the divine wrath; now would come the ultimate destruction. The sisters and their offspring would all die by the sword. Their previous sufferings and humiliations had not been enough; now God decreed death.

This destruction after painful punishment parallels the historical experience of Jerusalem. In 597 B.C.E., the Babylonian army had surrounded Jerusalem and taken many of its people into exile. Just a few years later, perhaps around 592 B.C.E., these exiles were in Babylonia, listening to Ezekiel's allegory and thinking about their former homeland. The exiles thought that maybe the punishment had been enough, that maybe they could return to their homeland and everything would be fine once more. Ezekiel prods them with anger and pain to realize that they will never go home again. At this point, Ezekiel affirms that complete destruction is about to come to Jerusalem. Within a few years, in 587 B.C.E., Babylonia completed their absolute destruction of Jerusalem, leaving nothing but a few burned shells. After punishment comes more punishment, until the destruction is complete.

The entire allegory ends with Ezekiel's familiar phrase: "and now you shall know that I am Yahweh God" (23:49). After this story, what does it mean to know Yahweh? Yahweh is the one who remains in control but who does not use powers of divine intervention to change events. The Babylonians bring the punishment to its climax, and God will not prevent it. Strangely, God is passive in all of this, providing Babylonia with tacit support for its policies. Other prophets may claim that God works through other nations to perform the divine will in the world, but Ezekiel stops short of that statement here. Still, God allows Babylonian destruction and claims that the people deserve the punishment that befalls them. Of course, these exiles in Ezekiel's audience will be the ones who survive the destruction of Jerusalem, because they have already been taken away from it. Others would die; the exiles would only lose their ancestral homes.

Perhaps this passage says one other thing about knowing God. In Hebrew, the verb "to know" can also refer to sexual intimacy. The inhabitants of Jerusalem have chosen to "know"

Assyria and Babylonia, and Ezekiel portrays this political collaboration in explicit sexual terms. Instead, God insists on receiving the people's knowledge and intimacy. Only once the people realize how violently destructive their association with other nations can be will they turn to Yahweh and truly know God. But this paints such a bleak picture of human existence, if it is true that people can only come to God through such pain. Perhaps we do better if we read this text as a stark reminder of the consequences of not knowing God, but even then we run risks of misunderstanding. This truly is a dangerous allegory.

The Allegory's Point

As in the previous chapters, Ezekiel strives to convince the exiles that Jerusalem will be destroyed, that they cannot return to their old home under any circumstances. Exile is permanent, and the people must learn to live in their new situation. In addition to the political and social problems that Jerusalem's destruction causes for the exiles, there is also a theological problem, as we have seen since Ezekiel's first chapter. The Babylonians have made a loud boast: they win wars because their god Marduk is the only real god, or at least is the most powerful of the gods. But how can that be? The Israelites believed for centuries that their Yahweh was the only God or at least the most powerful God; that was why they could win battles against other nations, or so they thought. If Yahweh lets Jerusalem lose, how can Yahweh be a god at all?

Ezekiel struggles with this question. His answer seems to lie at the root of this chapter and much of the rest of his prophecy. Yahweh is God, and all the exiles should know that with certainty, but that does not mean that God saves. God lets the nation of Judah lose its independence because the nation has sinned horribly, and deserves its destruction. The absence of Yahweh's intervention in international politics, then, becomes the *proof* of God's continued involvement with the chosen people, even though that involvement now takes the form of punishment. For Ezekiel, this is the point of the allegory: God's presence is perceived in punishment. The lack of salvation is the most certain substantiation of God's abiding existence.

The Problem with the Story

Ezekiel makes a peculiar, paradoxical point about punishment as proof of God's presence. In order to communicate such a strange message, Ezekiel uses powerful images that shock and distress the hearer and the reader. Such radically new ideas require odd and forceful images, but the unreasoning violence of this allegory seems to transgress even the wide-ranging bounds of this need. It is difficult to justify these images of rape, abuse, mutilation, and abandonment as portrayals of God's nature. Truly, we should not try to justify them.

What does require our attention, then? We need to focus on how Ezekiel interprets the historical events. He offers many interpretations, and since they are metaphors, they do not correspond exactly to the situations. Metaphors emphasize one part of the situation while often misconstruing another; the clarity they offer is a matter of focus. Allegories represent reality from a particular perspective. They interpret that reality and present a specific view to the audience. Allegories are never neutral; they always try to persuade the reader of their own opinion. Likewise, allegories are never perfect representations of reality, because of their bias. Allegories show parts of reality by distorting other parts. The allegory itself is not real; it points to truth and reality, as any effective fiction does.[6]

---

[6] Fiction is an appropriate mode of knowing truth, even though our culture and our church does not emphasize its importance. Jesus' parables provide an example of truth communicated in fictional stories. Though the good Samaritan and the other characters of Jesus' parables may never have actually existed and performed the actions of which Jesus tells, the point of the parable is still the same, and the story imparts truth through the mode of fiction.

Allegories also teach audiences about themselves. Through allegories and other metaphors, we come to a realization of who we are. In this allegory, the imagery forces us to uncover parts of our selves that we hesitate to see. We find our own willingness to blame the victim, to claim that it was all her fault and her responsibility, that she should be punished for what she did. We discover our own misogyny, our own culturally learned disrespect of women. Learning this about ourselves should give us reason to pause and to consider our own complicity in stories like this, as women and as men.

The imagery of this allegory should instill in us a negative reaction. It disturbs us to see such violence against women, and it *should* disturb us. It distresses us to hear a statement about God as one who abuses and murders one spouse after another. It should distress us deeply. We cannot afford to ignore that we too live in a society where such depictions of God can make sense, where women are still treated in that way, and where God seems to support this violence.

Our own stories must claim loudly that God cares for the victim. Surely this is Ezekiel's point, if we read widely enough. Throughout the book as a whole we learn that God desires that the chosen people be restored, that they be made whole again after Babylonia has violated them with such terror and violence. In this story it seems that we see God cheering on these horrors of abuse; if so, we must know with certainty that we see such things because our vision is so sharply limited. In reality, beyond the limits and distortions endemic to any allegory, God's care extends to the victims, and Yahweh will enfold each with love.

Responsibility and Punishment

In this painful allegory, human responsibility appears in striking form. The women Oholah and Oholibah are responsible for their deeds, and God holds them responsible, presiding over their punishment. But this imagery proves problematic for us, because of the painful portrait of God it provides.

I think that Ezekiel, whether intentionally or not, portrays for us the problem with his own thinking. We often think that the person responsible for a problem deserves punishment. In that line of thought, responsibility and punishment run together—the guilty, responsible party receives the punishment, and those who have been punished are assumed to have been guilty for some action, responsible for some sort of damage to humanity. But responsibility and punishment are not the same thing. Too often we confuse them. Suffering people are not necessarily guilty. God calls us into responsibility so that we may join in partnership, participating in the real work of creation with our Creator. God does not give us responsibility to test us or to manufacture reasons to punish us, but only in order to provide for us this opportunity to share our efforts with God's. When we fail our responsibility, that means that there is still more work to do; it does not necessarily mean that we deserve punishment for failing.

In similar fashion, God has made us responsible for the world, but that does not mean that we should be punished for the world's sins. Such views of God are too limited. We know that God desires to work with the world in the solution of its problems, but that partnership means that God needs us as willing participants in the divine labors of salvation. Punishment is counterproductive, and our viewing of violent punishment in places such as Ezekiel's allegory should only serve to help us reject those notions. We cannot allow ourselves to think that we have all responsibility, even though we carry a great deal. That is a great sin of pride. God is responsible, too. God provides ways for salvation, though they are at times so difficult to see.

7

Punishment for the Nations

(Ezekiel 25—32)

In Ezekiel 1—24, the prophet's chief concerns have focused on God's plans for the exiles and for Jerusalem. This represents the earliest years of the exile, when many of the Jews still thought that they might return to Jerusalem. Judah was struggling to make alliances with Egypt that would stave off the threats of Babylonia, allowing Judah to regain true independence. Ezekiel's message was that Babylonia would destroy Jerusalem completely, no matter what they did, and that the exiles would stay in Babylonia permanently. For the next several chapters, Ezekiel's prophecy widens to include a broader international perspective.

In these chapters, the readers discover that Yahweh is globally concerned. Other nations believed in other gods, each of whom were local deities. Marduk, god of the Babylonians, served the people nearby, and Marduk's worshipers knew that

their god could have no effect except locally. It was the same
for the other national gods. But Yahweh was a truly international deity, with concerns and plans all over the world. For
this reason, Yahweh's prophet utters sayings that deal with the
fate of the rest of the world. These oracles against the nations
take the same critical perspectives that Ezekiel uses to discuss
the exile's concerns and applies them to the global political
situation. Yahweh was working in many places on a multina-
tional scale to accomplish the divine will.

Through these oracles against the nations, Ezekiel expresses
the proper context for his earlier discussion of the punishment
of Jerusalem. Ezekiel's exilic audience needed to understand
God's wider purposes in order to interpret properly what they
saw happening all around them. God's plans are large and
long, and require the knowledge of the whole world. Though
the exiles formed God's chosen people, there were still other
concerns around them, and God's interests surpassed the welfare of just one small nation. As a later prophet said, all the
earth is God's footstool (Isaiah 66:1). The entire globe forms
the stage where all of us are actors, and God directs the whole
production.

Oracles Against the Nations

The oracles against the nations were not a new phenom-
enon for Ezekiel. This form of prophetic speech had appeared
as early as two centuries before the exile, in the preaching and
writing of other prophets. The book of Amos begins with
oracles against all of Israel's immediate neighbors, climaxing
with a stunning critique of Israel itself. Isaiah and Jeremiah
both spend large portions of their prophecy focusing on the
situations of other nations. In that sense, there is nothing
unique about Ezekiel's international concerns.

What is striking is that Ezekiel covers very few nations.
After a short list at the beginning, Tyre and Egypt combine for
about 90 percent of Ezekiel's oracles against the nations. This
prophet never offers a comprehensive listing of the interna-

tional situation; he provides deeper analyses of two specific geopolitical circumstances and short mentions of some others.

The beginning overview lists four of Judah's near neighbors: Ammon, Moab, Edom, and Philistia. Ammon, to Jerusalem's east, receives condemnation for plundering portions of Judah in the wake of the first Babylonian invasion; their punishment will be the loss of their land. Moab, to the southeast, committed the same crimes and receives the same sentence. God sentences death for Edom, Judah's southern neighbor, because of their taking revenge against Judah. Finally, God will kill the cities of Philistia, which was on the coast west of Judah, in revenge for their malice. With these short oracles out of the way, Ezekiel turns to his lengthier concerns.

Tyre (26:1—28:24)

Tyre was a great city on a small island, just off the eastern Mediterranean coast, about one hundred miles north of Jerusalem. Often called Phoenicia, Tyre was an important maritime power throughout most of Israel's history. It controlled the shipping lanes and the merchant marine traffic for a large area, including Israel, Judah, and the rest of Palestine, and as far west and north as Cyprus and even Greece. This constant traffic and trade enabled Tyre to become a powerful and often selfish city, influencing the peoples and the economies around them with a careless abandon. Because of their position, power, and wealth, many other nations both envied and hated Tyre, and these attitudes certainly arise in Ezekiel's prophecies about that northern seaport.

Babylonia and Tyre (26:1–21)

A simple, unadorned statement in the middle of this prophecy provides the core: "Thus says Lord Yahweh: I will bring against Tyre from the north King Nebuchadrezzar of Babylon, king of kings, together with horses, chariots, cavalry, and a

great and powerful army" (26:7). In short, Ezekiel prophesies
Tyre's destruction in ways that are very similar to Jerusalem's
own devastation by Babylonia.[1]

But this core offers only the most minimalist description of
Ezekiel's prophecy, because in the rest of this chapter, Ezekiel
uses exquisite poetry to convey Tyre's destruction. The prophecy begins with the words of Yahweh the plunderer: "Shattered
are the gates of the peoples. They have swung open to me, and
I shall be filled with its waste" (26:2). Tyre had long styled
itself as a gateway to the world, as do many port cities and
transportation hubs even today. Because Tyre brought the
world to the doors of people who could not afford to travel, it
enjoyed a special position in the minds of its inhabitants and
neighbors, but now Babylonian military might sweeps away
that privilege. With the warehouses of the port city broken
open, anyone can come and replenish wealth by plundering
and looting the demolished city. The prophecy uses maritime
language to describe ironically Tyre's fate: many nations will
crash against its walls like waves, and the city itself will become
a flat place, a place for spreading nets as fishers do (26:3–5).

Ezekiel describes in grim detail the process of a siege as the
Babylonian army had perfected (26:8–12). First, the army
invaded the unprotected suburban areas (called "daughter cities") and killed the entire populace. Then they constructed a
large, thin wall around the wall that surrounded the city itself.
From this wall the army directed its arrows and other weapons
against Tyre, and they built ramps down which the army
poured into the besieged city. With battering rams, the army

---

[1] It is striking that Babylonia receives mention only in this one verse.
Without this verse, one could not determine the nationality of the attack-
ing army from the sparse other clues presented. Combined with the recognition that Ezekiel 26:7 is a prosaic statement different from the poetry of
the rest of the oracles against Tyre, this has caused many scholars to suggest
that Ezekiel 26:1—28:19 were later additions to these prophecies. In that
case, almost all Ezekiel's oracles against the nations focus on Egypt, which is
quite understandable, and the Tyre oracles are early postexilic prophecies of
later troubles.

breached the walls and sent in troops on horseback in such numbers that they overwhelmed the inhabitants of the city, who had been weakened with hunger for months. Then the city's goods were plundered, the walls destroyed, the buildings demolished. For a coastal town, the debris was pushed into the sea, making the task of rebuilding even more impossible. But these are events of the future, seen through the prophetic eye as if they were already happening.

When Tyre's destruction finally occurs, then the nations will take notice, and will realize the powers that had been brought against it. For months, maybe years, ships would sail into Tyre's harbors, looking to offload their goods from the corners of the earth, but they would find nothing, because the city's destruction had been so absolute. Nothing would be left for these weary travelers to find, and they would be left alone in the rubble, standing in amazement at the powers that could have destroyed such a strong, vibrant port.

Tyre's Former Wealth (27:1–36)

Next, Ezekiel moves into a discussion of Tyre's former wealth. He emphasizes the heights from which this city fell into destruction. This prophecy comes in the form of a lamentation, a mournful recalling of Tyre's grandeur that now is gone. It begins with Tyre's own claim: "I am perfect in beauty" (27:3). In a poem comparing the city to an expensive boat, we learn that the city's construction included the finest timber from throughout the region, inlaid with ivory, and that the peoples of Tyre had come from throughout the known world. Skilled archers in high towers protected the city from any threat. Tyre's trading partners stretched from Greece to Africa, from Asia Minor to Babylonia and Arabia, including all of the nations of Palestine, and the most exotic of metals, foods, horses, woods, spices, stones, and fabrics comprised their rich, abundant commerce. But then the destruction arrived, and all the goods and all the people disappeared utterly from the face of the earth, as if they were sinking into the sea.

When the destruction came, Tyre's mariners stood on the shore and cried over their loss, tearing out their hair and wailing aloud (27:28–31). They offered a haunting lamentation:

> Who was ever like Tyre
>   in the midst of the sea?
> When your wares came from the seas,
>   you satisfied many peoples;
> With the abundance of your wealth and merchandise,
>   you made rich the kings of the earth.
> Now you are shattered on the seas,
>   in the depths of the water;
> your merchandise and all your crew
>   have sunk while inside you.
> All the inhabitants of the coastlands
>   are appalled at you.
> Their king's hair stands on end;
>   their faces are haggard.
> The merchants among the peoples hiss at you.
> You have become a terror
>   and shall be no more forever.
>
> Ezekiel 27:32–36[2]

Those who watch Tyre's destruction or discover it afterward cry aloud in pain. They stand together on the shores and watch the emptiness that once was a thriving city. All the other cities nearby wallow in horror and fear, in no small part because they know that Tyre's fate could befall them next. If Babylonia can ravage Tyre, then their army can destroy anyone.

The Pride of Tyre's King (28:1–10)

Ezekiel's prophecy against Tyre now takes a more personal approach and condemns the ruler of Tyre. This prince was proud, comparing himself to a god. True, the prince of Tyre

---

[2] For the translational difficulties in this poem, see Walther Zimmerli, *Ezekiel 2* (Hermeneia; Philadelphia: Fortress Press, 1983), pp. 52–53.

was widely known for great wisdom, as well as for immense personal wealth, but this great human achievement was nothing compared to the approaching army. Thus, Yahweh has a question for the prince of Tyre: "Will you still say, 'I am a god,' in the presence of those who kill you?" (28:9). The prince's great splendor that bordered on the divine had a limit: he was still mortal.

Perhaps it is not too much to read into these words a critique of Judah. The ruling classes of Jerusalem could have possessed the same pride in themselves, in their wealth, and in their wisdom. But these pretensions would never be enough to keep out the armies that would destroy the city and exile its inhabitants. To lift oneself up as a god is a sin of pride that leads to destruction, but Ezekiel is hardly advocating dependence upon the military might that could oppose the Babylonian army. Even the people who correctly believe in God find their home cities destroyed, and they themselves are forced to live in exile. In the face of the world's greatest army, belief does not keep you alive, in the same way that wisdom and wealth are never enough to keep the army at bay.

The Wisdom of Tyre's King (28:11–19)

Ezekiel's second prophetic condemnation of Tyre's leader focuses more explicitly on the wisdom and beauty of the king. Tyre was a wonderful place of great beauty and primeval wisdom, comparable to Eden but constructed with the most exotic manufactured materials. But once Yahweh found sin in the hearts of the Eden-dwellers, God threw them out, and destruction was at hand. Tyre died by fire, the flames quenching the pride of the king. All the world watched and was appalled, again because they knew that destruction could come upon anyone if it could destroy the wealth and beauty of Tyre.

At the end of all Ezekiel's words about Tyre, this one point arises above the rest. Tyre's fall is something for all the nations to watch, a lesson from which the whole world can learn. This should not be surprising, because the prophet delivered this oracle, like all of the oracles against the nations, to the exiles in Babylonia, not to Tyre itself. It would not be helpful to encourage change in Tyre's behavior that might lead to salvation, if Tyre would never hear the message. Instead, the exiles can learn more about God's will from this oracle. God intends that all nations receive their due for the haughtiness of their leadership. Yahweh does not single out Judah for punishment; what happens to Judah is merely part of God's wider activity in the world. This global context provides a basis for the exiles' proper interpretation of their situation.

Interlude: A Blessing for Israel (28:25–26)

In between the two main sections of Ezekiel's oracles against the nations, the prophet offers a very brief blessing for Israel. In some future day, God will gather those who have been scattered from Judah and return them to their land. In their own nation once more, they shall live in safety and prosperity, watching while God executes punishment upon the nations of the world that have treated the Jews poorly.

This note of future blessing complements the oracles against the other nations, but it also contradicts it. The oracles emphasize that all the world receives the same care and activity from Yahweh, but this blessing promises special, favorable treatment for Judah. For this reason, it is very important to read this blessing in the context of the oracles. Without the oracles' negativity ringing in our ears, we might hear privilege in this blessing and think that Judah is somehow God's favorite nation, not held to the same rules as the world. Set here in the midst of the oracles, we can be reminded that God's vision includes the whole world, and that God's chosen ones of Judah play but a small part on that global stage.

Egypt (29:1—32:32)

Though the oracles against Tyre come first in the current book of Ezekiel, the oracles against Egypt hold the earlier date by at least a few months.[3] These oracles originate in 587 B.C.E. At that time, the Babylonian forces were rampant in the area of the Mediterranean. The army was in the middle of its fatal siege of Jerusalem, and the lengthy siege of Tyre was just starting. Egypt's destruction seemed only months away. As in previous parts of Ezekiel's book, Egypt holds a special place in the prophet's attention. In these years between the beginning of the exile and the complete destruction of Jerusalem, there were close connections between Judah and Egypt, as they schemed together to prevent the Babylonians from taking the rest of Palestine. However, their plots were in vain, as Ezekiel had known they would be. In Babylonia, Ezekiel could see the strength of their vast armies, and he knew that even Judah and even Egypt would have no chance for victory against them. If Egypt battled Babylonia, Egypt would attain the same utter destruction that awaited Judah.

When Ezekiel prophesies against Egypt in the hearing of the exiles, he warns these Babylonian Jews that reliance upon Egypt would come to no good. There were no possible ways to resist Babylonia, and thus they should not try.

Pharaoh the Fish and the Destruction of Egypt (29:1—30:26)

According to this oracle, Egypt's Pharaoh was like a great dragon, a sea serpent of enormous proportions living in the Nile River, possessing it as a lair. But Yahweh is a fisher, casting a line for this huge fish, catching it with hooks in its jaws. God does not bother to skin and filet this fish for eating; it is a worthless fish, flung into a field where it flops and dies, feeding the birds with its rotting flesh. Its life is not worth anything, and its destruction is complete. Then all the inhabitants of Egypt will know that Yahweh is God.

But the oracle continues in a surprising direction. Though Egypt has become a desolation, with its inhabitants scattered throughout the nations, God will wait forty years and then will

---

[3] For dates, see Moshe Greenberg, *Ezekiel 1–20* (Anchor Bible; Doubleday, 1983), pp. 8–11.

restore the people of Egypt, bringing them together from the ends of the earth. Though Egypt will be a small nation in those new days, it will exist again. At least its people are restored, even if they suffer the fate of a small nation, as Israel and Judah had always been. Because Egypt will be so insignificant in those days, no other nation will rely on her, as Judah did in its last days, but Egypt will be a nation again. Quite surprisingly, God blesses Egypt and restores its inhabitants as a nation, giving them the same promises given to Judah. They too shall know Yahweh as their savior. This remarkable salvation of Egypt goes against so many of the expectations of these oracles, which usually envision the enduring destruction of other peoples, but it expresses Ezekiel's far-reaching vision that God's salvation carries into the world.

Just as Judah's promised restoration awaits a future day, so does Egypt's. In the meantime, Egypt will suffer even more. God gives this nation over to the Babylonians, who will plunder it in order to finance their military adventures. Not only does Egypt suffer the travesties of defeat, but it also faces the ignominy of paying for its own destruction. Such is the fate of wealthy nations.

When the armies come, all of Egypt will experience destruction, including all of Egypt's surrounding territories. God's wrath extends especially to the Egyptian cities and to the images of the other gods worshiped there. Pharaoh will fall to the strength of King Nebuchadrezzar of Babylonia, and all the Egyptians will march off into exile throughout the world (30:20–26).

The Trees of God's Garden (31:1–18)

In an exquisite poem, Ezekiel asks Pharaoh how great he thinks he is. To whom can he compare himself? Yahweh asks Pharaoh to consider the mighty Assyrians. They were like a lofty cedar tree, with great heights in its branches and remarkable depths to its thick roots. This tree gave shade to many birds and animals; it was a center of life for the forest around it. None of the other trees could compare to it at all, for size or for beauty. But this Assyrian tree became proud, and so God sent Babylonia to cut it down. Never again should trees reach to the heavens.[4] Now God sends the challenge to Egypt. Egypt was another of the largest trees, and so comes its time and Babylonia will chop it down, too. Like a great tree felled in the forest, Babylonia will bring Egypt down to the ground.[5]

The Graves of the Nations (32:1–32)

Again Yahweh presses the point home: Babylonia will defeat Egypt with awesome military might and will carry off Egypt's inhabitants into exile, those whom the sword does not immediately kill. Deep in the pit called Sheol, Egypt will lie down in its grave, surrounded by the graves of the other great nations destroyed by Babylonia. In deep lamentation, Ezekiel reads off the list of the graves of the nations: Assyria, Elam, Meshech, Tubal, Edom, Sidon, and now Egypt (32:22–30). Ironically, the sight makes Pharaoh glad; at last he knows that he did not die alone, but that he was conquered only by the unstoppable force of the new world power, Babylonia.

Ezekiel delivers this message less than two months after he has learned that Babylonia had breached Jerusalem's gates and completed their destruction of Judah (33:21–22). With respectable insight, Ezekiel reasons that Babylonia will never be beaten, and that their devastation will continue to sweep southward until Egypt too meets its match and reaches its end. Surprisingly, Ezekiel was wrong. Babylonia never conquered Egypt, nor made a serious attempt to attack Egypt. The Babylonian Empire seemed to rest after the destruction of Judah and its surrounding territories, comfortable in the fact that only Egypt remained as a challenge and that there was a vast buffer zone between the imperial core and the distant land

---

[4] Ezekiel may well be borrowing from the Tower of Babel tradition (Genesis 11).

[5] In the Old Testament, God often uses other nations as instruments of the divine will.

of Egypt; Judah was one of the furthest outposts in that buffer zone.[6]

Despite the fact that Ezekiel was wrong in predicting a Babylonian conquest of Egypt, he maintained this position and the passage remained in the records of his prophetic words. Prophecies are not predictions that God promises to make come true; they are insightful interpretations of God's will in everyday life. Ezekiel reached to deeper truths in these oracles. He knew how unstoppable Babylonia had become and that all of its enemies fell to a common grave. Resistance to the Empire was foolish. Though Ezekiel misinterpreted the exact ramifications of Babylonian dominance, he understood God's will for Judah with startling clarity, arguing against the interpretations that most of his contemporaries offered. They argued that Egypt could be Judah's salvation, but Ezekiel insisted on the futility of reliance upon Egypt: only Yahweh would ever be Judah's salvation.

For this reason, we can readily understand one of Ezekiel's most surprising moves. Typically, a list of oracles against the nations would include condemnations of every major international force. But Ezekiel never condemns the true enemy, Babylonia. Undoubtedly, this serves the prophet's purpose, which is to prove that Babylonia is the agent of God's will in the world. There should be no condemnation of Babylonia because Ezekiel strives to convince Judah's exile of their own complicity. To indict Babylonia would only serve to pass the blame onto other nations, and this Ezekiel continually refuses.

The God of the Whole World

When the word of Jerusalem's destruction comes to Ezekiel, he finds himself unable to speak (33:21–22). Yahweh then

---

[6] Later, the Persian Empire defeated Egypt, and Ezekiel's prophecies may have been reinterpreted to speak of Cambyses' or Darius' conquests of Egypt. For this time period, see Jon L. Berquist, *In Persia's Shadow: The Beginnings of Second Temple Judah* (Minneapolis, Minnesota: Fortress Press, forthcoming). However, the text of Ezekiel clearly and repeatedly refers to Babylonia as the conqueror.

explains to the prophet that not only will Jerusalem meet its end, but the surrounding areas will become a wasteland as well. Those who hide there will die by the sword, hunted by Babylonian soldiers until those warriors find them and kill them. Still, the exiles strive to see some benefit for themselves in these events, but God cautions Ezekiel that they will never understand the true distress that has come their way.

History went in a different direction. Many more people survived in Jerusalem and the surrounding vicinity than Ezekiel could have guessed. Of course, none of the rich and powerful survived in the land. This seems to be the situation with which Ezekiel concerned himself. Many of the Jews survived in and near Jerusalem, but the political entity of Judah did not regain its power. As far as Ezekiel told the people, Yahweh was no longer the God of Jerusalem, but was now the God of the exiles near Nippur, in the heart of Babylonia.

But we keep hearing of God's activity elsewhere. Yahweh controlled the outcomes of the Babylonian army's various battles, and directed the fate of Egypt, Tyre, and many other nations. These events proved God's presence in the world in striking ways. God's willingness to save Egypt in forty years, just as God had saved Israel and would again save the exiles, proves that the nature of God continues through time. God is still present; God is still God; God is still caring and loving; and above all, God is still responsible. God's responsibility carries with it the purging of the nations. Israel is not alone in the punishment it experiences; they must not think that they were singled out by a wrathful, vengeful God.

God is a global God, concerned with the affairs of many nations. God's concerns go far past the Israelites. The world has many problems, and they must all be treated. The problems must be found and removed, with force if necessary. God is a physician who must operate in the world to save it, and at times that means that God saves us from ourselves by removing parts that would harm us, even if those parts are parts of ourselves. This large-scale, full-bodied, global perspective becomes the only perspective wide enough to assist in our understanding of God.

Similarly, God's people of today are not alone in the world. God's concerns are still global, and they stop at nothing less than taking away the sins of the world. We have always been invited to be God's partners in this process of removing sin, but we must also face the fact that we are sinners, too, just as the rest of the world is. The international, global perspectives are vital for the church of today, especially when we consider the ways in which we might be the problem, instead of part of God's solution. The divine surgeon may need to operate here as well, but God would rather have us as partners instead of patients, if we are willing. To do so, we must see the big picture of God's actions throughout the world. If our vision is too narrow, we have no sense of mission, and we may fall into the exiles' trap of bemoaning our own fate. Yahweh is a global God, and we are not alone in God's sight.

8

Shepherds

(Ezekiel 34)

Once again, Ezekiel takes up the issue of human responsibility, but with a new emphasis. The prophet focuses now
upon the responsibilities of the leaders. In the previous chapters, Ezekiel has discussed responsibility in general terms, making
no distinction between the various types of responsibility held
by different persons within the community. Here, his presentation moves into new ground, thinking about the special kinds
of responsibility that accompany leadership.

In chapter 34, Ezekiel falls short of a true allegory, but he
does extensively develop the metaphor of leaders as shepherds
and followers as sheep. This is a familiar metaphor in the Bible.
Both Old Testament and New Testament passages describe
leadership with this rural image. Throughout biblical times,
people would have been more familiar with the life and work
of a shepherd than modern people are. Many of the ancients

were shepherds or had shepherds in the family, and this fact of society provided an extensive base of experience to support the use of this metaphor. Though shepherding is not nearly as prevalent today, it is still a common vocation, well represented in popular stories, if not directly in people's experience. In many ways, the situation today parallels Ezekiel's audience. Although shepherding was much more common in his day, his audience of exiles was mostly upper class, and not many of them would have been shepherds themselves. They may have disparaged shepherding as a task beneath their own social status. But still they knew what shepherds did, with at least enough familiarity to understand Ezekiel's metaphor without any hesitancy.

In this chapter Ezekiel thinks mostly of political and religious leadership, reflecting on the conditions of Judah a few years earlier that resulted in the exile. The absolute, final destruction of Jerusalem was a few years prior, in Ezekiel's immediate past, and the community in exile was gradually growing accustomed to their loss. Even though a few years had passed, these exiles were still concentrating their thought and discussion in an attempt to determine the reasons why the exile had occurred. They sought explanations for this tragic event that had shocked and altered their lives. Most of all, they may have searched for people to blame. Whose fault was the exile?

Many of the people listening to Ezekiel had been Jerusalem's leaders, as were most of the Jews living in exile. Babylonia had deported the city's leaders, and Ezekiel's audience of exiles was an audience of former leaders. If they were typical humans, they may well have tried to put the blame on other people. The politicians might have blamed the priests; the priests might have blamed the politicians; and both groups might have blamed the common people of Jerusalem, who should have listened to their leaders but who refused. "If only the commoners had done what we told them to do," they would argue, "we never would have been in this situation." For the commoners' sin, God killed them, and this exile became the leaders' punishment, according to this line of thinking.

Though the political and religious leaders may have thought this way, Ezekiel provides a different solution. He suggests that the issue of blame is not so simple, but that the blame first rests with those in positions of authority. This message would not have been popular at all, but it would expand the understandings of the exiles, encouraging them to see all the factors involved in the destruction of Jerusalem. Above all, this metaphor would help the leaders to see how they had contributed to their own disaster. Ezekiel encouraged them to accept responsibility themselves. But, of course, they were not the only ones to blame. The situation, as is so often the case, was never that simple.

Shepherds and Leaders (34:1–16)

Gaining Advantage from Leading (34:1–6)

The passage begins with an examination of the wrong sort of leaders, depicted as poor shepherds. God harshly condemned unfaithful leaders. The issue was the kind of care these leaders provided for their flocks. The shepherds that Ezekiel described had been taking care of themselves instead of giving the appropriate care to their flocks. Selfishness and greed were their motivations, and so they did not respond to the legitimate needs of their flocks. These shepherds fed themselves instead of feeding their sheep. They saw their job as shepherd as merely a means to self-profit, and they did not understand their role as an opportunity for service.

Not only did these poor shepherds forget their task, but they actively worked against the best interest of their sheep. These shepherds ate their sheep! They ate the choice portions of the meat, and then clothed themselves with the wool. They concerned themselves only with the best of the flock, because those animals would prove most helpful to the shepherds. Any animals that were weak, crippled, or lost received no help from these shepherds, who were too busy chasing their own profits to pursue a lost lamb. Suffering from this neglect combined with abuse, the flock scattered. Without protection or even the solidarity of the flock, the sheep wandered, facing the perils of starvation and attack by the wild beasts.

The Fate of the Shepherds (34:7–10)

Just like Jerusalem's political and religious leaders, the shepherds of this metaphorical field damaged their flock, taking from them their very lives to provide advantage for the powerful and disregarding the needs of the weak to maximize profit. But God will not be content to watch all this occur without taking action. God will not be passive while the shepherds damage the flock. Instead, God will rescue the sheep from the hands of the shepherds.

The changing references to the shepherds warrant attention. In the first reference, Yahweh addressed them directly as "you shepherds" (34:7); almost immediately they became the object of condemnation. Though Yahweh had appointed them, referring to them as "my shepherds" (34:8), suggesting that they were obligated to Yahweh to care for God's flock, Yahweh observed that they did not do the job. In the fields where the flock needed help, there was "no shepherd" (34:8). Because they failed at their divinely appointed tasks, Yahweh announced opposition to the shepherds (34:10). This resulted in the punishment: "no longer shall the shepherds feed themselves" (34:10). They will lose their source of advantage, which has given them food to eat and an ease of life for years.

The New Shepherd (34:11–16)

God will then take over the care of the sheep personally. Yahweh's first task as shepherd is to find the lost sheep, assuming the tasks that the worthless shepherds had failed to do. The rescue of lost sheep from throughout the world became God's primary goal. Ezekiel's use of the metaphor pointed to an end to the exile, when all of God's people would come together in Judah once more. The leaders, whom God removed from their positions as shepherds, were now sheep once more, and so they could be part of the saved community.

When Yahweh leads the flock, there is water for all, and also good pastures and rest from the heat of the day. This becomes a test for Yahweh's community and for the adequacy of the shepherds. God's human leaders should provide food and water for others, keeping them safe from hunger, from attack, and from overexertion. But shepherds do more than that; they are more than protective and preventive. Good shepherds seek the lost sheep, placing themselves at risk for the security of others; they all heal the crippled and strengthen the weak. These are the responsibilities of human leaders, if they would follow Yahweh's example as shepherd.

The Responsibility of the Leaders

If the leaders understood in Ezekiel 34 are the Jews exiled in Babylonia, who had served formerly as the leaders of Jerusalem, then this is a very radical passage. Their sin as leaders was in neglecting their sheep, the common folk of Judah. Their punishment was their removal from positions of leadership, which occurred through the exile of the leaders to Babylonia. But in a new day, Yahweh will care for all the sheep. Yahweh will call all the sheep from around the world together, back in Judah, and the exiles will be the sheep, not the shepherds. Only when the leaders cease being leaders and return to being sheep can they be saved.

What then is the responsibility of the leaders? The story offers two distinct answers. The first answer is that leaders are responsible to be the kind of shepherd that God is. God cares for the people in completely unselfish ways, looking out for their advantage and avoiding all ways to make profit off of the caring for others. Shepherds feed their flocks, taking them to places of water and safety, chasing after the lost and bringing them home, healing the hurting so that they can join into the community with full participation. Good shepherds never consider their own gain, but support the sheep in what they do best: eating and grazing and drinking and resting. Good shepherds respect their sheep and help them to be even better sheep. From these sorts of guidelines, humans can learn how to imitate God and thus how to be the right kind of shepherds.

But Ezekiel offers a second answer as well. When God removes from office the bad shepherds who have failed their tasks, God does not search for another generation of shepherds, thinking perhaps that better training could result in shepherds who were at least adequate. Instead, God chooses to become the shepherd and does the shepherds' tasks directly. God no longer requires human leaders. This is a stunning critique of the whole idea of human leadership in God's name. This passage from the prophet Ezekiel can provide a powerful model for relativizing the importance of leaders. We must not think that we *need* human leaders; we have God.[1] Leadership must never replace God; God replaces dependence upon human leaders.

This critique perhaps goes too far. Certainly, the text hints at two answers that are wildly divergent and even contradictory, but possibly the text also offers a middle response. The primary work of caring for humanity is God's task. Others can join in *partnership* with God, but the partnership has its limits. As God's partners, we cannot define the task; God has already defined it and we must agree with it to continue as partners. The task of caring for people is non-negotiable in this partnership. When we humans work on the task of caring, God works through us. The best caring occurs when God and people work together to provide for the needs of people! But this is not quite leadership, at least not in the senses we often think. We are God's partners, working on the agenda God gives us. This caring is the type of shepherding to which God calls us humans; this is the only type of "leadership" that is appropriate. God is the true shepherd, and we also are shepherds when we join in God's tasks as partners.

---

[1] Cp. the discussion of Israel's monarchy in 1 Samuel 8. This text shows the debate between the need for effective human leadership and the view that God is the true king, the true leader of the people Israel.

God's Continuing Shepherding

The image of God as shepherd is a powerfully evocative expression of God's care and concern for people. Thus, it comes as no surprise that this image finds itself used repeatedly to talk about God's desire to care for people. When Zechariah 11 talks of the damaging leadership of that prophet's time, those poor leaders are compared to worthless shepherds, who shatter grace and lead their sheep to slaughter. Ezekiel's metaphorical shepherd language was rich enough to empower many instances with prophetic potential.

Luke 15:3–7 contains one of Jesus' parables, in which Jesus asks, "Who would not go after a lost sheep, no matter how many were owned? And when the sheep is found, who would not come back with rejoicing?" To this person bringing home a lost sheep, Jesus compares a single repentant sinner and the joy of heaven. God's concerns for the lost is strong, and God always moves into the forefront of those who seek for the lost. God continues on until the last sheep can return home safely. God's care extends throughout the whole community, not only to those who need little care or to those who are attractive and beneficial. For God, the greatest joy comes in the sheep that is hardest to find, the sheep that has run the farthest from the fold.

In the Gospel of John, Jesus again uses the image of a shepherd (John 10:1–18). Other shepherds have come before Jesus, but they had taken advantage of the flock, just as the early shepherds in Ezekiel 34 had done. Jesus, however, truly cares for the flock and does what is best for them. As Jesus explains, the other shepherds seek to take life, but Jesus seeks to give life to the sheep, with complete free will. Jesus learns from God's example, as recorded in Ezekiel 34, and becomes the right kind of shepherd for the people.

Sheep and Followers (34:17–31)

If God is shepherd and we are God's partners in the caring of the world, then who are the sheep of the flock? Ezekiel's metaphor continues to focus increasingly upon the sheep.

Caring for the Pasture (34:17–19)

The readers' expectations at this point in Ezekiel's metaphorical story are straightforward. The story contains shepherds and sheep, and in the opening scenes, the reader sees the evils perpetrated by the shepherds, causing the sheep to suffer severely and unjustly. Then Yahweh enters and takes the responsibility away from the shepherds, chastising them for their poor performance and their greedy selfishness. Next, Yahweh pledges to take good care of the sheep. When Yahweh begins to speak about the sheep, the reader expects the sheep to be blessed, and perhaps to be comforted in recompense for the suffering they experienced at the hands of evil shepherds. But the readers' expectations are suddenly shattered: God holds the sheep accountable for their deeds as well!

These sheep have not been blameless. While feeding, they have trampled down the grass so that others could not eat. When drinking, they fouled the water so others could not drink. They did not conserve their resources so that the pastures and streams would provide for the most people possible. Instead, in their unthinking greed, these sheep used what they needed without caring for the other sheep. For this, God criticizes them.

Though there is strong responsibility placed on the shoulders of the leaders, the followers (Ezekiel's sheep) are also responsible for their work. There is work for the sheep, too! They must care for their resources and be sure that there is enough for everyone to eat and drink. The sheep must shepherd their resources carefully, just as they are shepherded with caring provision.

An ecological interpretation would not be out of place here. The care for our surroundings is properly our task. This passage phrases its environmental issues without resorting to notions of sacrifice; the key issue is *not* what we give up. These sheep feed, and they feed well under the care of their shepherd; God does not call them to sacrifice their own needs in order to meet the needs of others. But the sheep are aware of the inadvertent effects of their own actions, and they should be careful that they do not use up the resources that others need to eat. In this vision, there can be enough food and enough resources for all the sheep, but those who come to the pasture first must be careful that they do not sully what rightfully belongs to others.

Caring for the Flock (34:20–24)

Two new ideas enlarge the sheep metaphor with the next passage: a note of judgment and an announcement of a new shepherd. Both of these elements work against some of the notions developed earlier; they serve as needed correctives to our interpretations of the metaphor as a whole.

Judgment comes against the fat sheep. They have pushed their way to the front of the line at the feeding troughs; they have elbowed their companion sheep out of the most abundant pastures and into sparser ground. For this sin of greed promoted by power, the fat sheep receive judgment. This assists in our own interpretation of the previous ecological themes. We earlier read that we must be sure not to trample the food of others; now we know also to take our own place in line, making sure that others have a fair share of the pasture. If we give the other sheep enough food to live, but we grow fat while they stay lean, then we earned judgment. Instead, we must make sure that the food and the pastureland itself is equally distributed; God desires no fat sheep and no lean sheep. Ecology and the feeding of the hungry are rightfully parts of the same concern, and both of them are central to the faith that Yahweh desires.

Second, God announces a new shepherd, helping us to think more about the problems of human leadership and Ezekiel's twin answers to that question. God appoints as shepherd a servant, David. David was the classic shepherd-boy turned warrior-king of the books of Samuel; his long reign as Israel's second king saw the development of the monarchy in much of its later trappings. In Ezekiel's prophecy, however,

David never appears as king, but only as shepherd; he also receives the title *nasî*. Though *nasî* is typically translated as "prince," or sometimes as "chief," its true meaning is more limited. A *nasî* is a leader, and as leader the specific tasks of the *nasî* vary. Certainly, a *nasî* is not a king, with all the power and prestige of that royal office.

David appears in this passage, but without his royal trappings. Suddenly, this David returns to his humble roots, serving again as a simple shepherd and receiving a title much less than those of his years as monarch. He is not king; he is merely *nasî*. In this role, he cares for the flock. No special respect or honor is due to David; his work seems to be his reward. For such a striking statement that seems to verge on messianic thinking, Ezekiel gives surprisingly little attention to this notion of a shepherd like David, but the possibility that a human can actually serve as shepherd grows in clarity throughout the passage. Humans can serve as God's partners, but only when they refuse the trappings of leadership that we humans so often place upon our leaders, such as monarchy. Only the hardworking servant will function as a shepherd. In this context, it is important that the Hebrew word *'ebed*, translated as servant, is also the word for slave. God's shepherd will not be an independent thinker, but one whose will and mind and actions are completely in line with Yahweh's own intentions. The person who is one with Yahweh can serve as a slave does, in the role of leader or shepherd.

Covenant of Peace and Prosperity (34:25–31)

In a final blessing, Yahweh speaks of a day when there will be *shalom* for the sheep. The meaning of *shalom* as "peace" has become rather common in today's churches, but *shalom* means more than "peace." It also means "prosperity," though not in the sense most familiar to us. We too often think of prosperity as overabundance; we become prosperous only when we have more possessions than we can possibly use. In God's vision, the prosperity of *shalom* occurs when everyone has enough; in the prosperous nation, *everyone* receives food, clothing, shelter, care, and provision, and there is no lack. Prosperity happens not when a few people have more than everyone else, but when everyone has exactly enough, measured by God's standards.[2]

Of course, *shalom* also means peace, both the cessation of violence and the presence of sensitive, caring cooperation. Peace and prosperity belong together in *shalom*. When there is prosperity, then there is little cause for hostility. When people care for each other in peace, the fair and equal distribution of resources comes naturally. When this *shalom* comes to our community, we will know that Yahweh is God, because our community will bespeak the very nature of God. We will be God's people; Yahweh will be our God; and we will be the sheep of God's own pasture.

Leaders and Followers

In God's vision we are sheep, and Yahweh is the shepherd. Human leadership is possible, but we do best when we follow God in providing for others. The only path to true leadership is through following God. Ecology and economy combine within God's concerns, because both affect the welfare of the sheep. God wants us as shepherds and as sheep, because both are roles of caring for God's people.

The responsibility of leadership forms an important issue for the contemporary church. Maintaining high standards of responsibility for our church leaders is essential. But other issues are also present. It is the responsibility of the church to do the work of God, and thus the sheep are responsible for the character of the shepherds. The church is God's flock, and the leaders assume no special relationship with God. For a priest, Ezekiel was strongly anti-clerical, because the work of God must be done by the people—not by the leaders. Leaders fail, and the church must hold them accountable because the church

---

[2] See the notions of abundance and sufficiency as developed in Jon L. Berquist, *Ancient Wine, New Wineskins: The Lord's Supper in Old Testament Perspective* (St. Louis, Missouri: Chalice Press, 1991), chapter 3.

holds a higher responsibility. But in the end, the ultimate responsibility belongs to God, and God upholds that responsibility in ways that eventually bring peace and prosperity to all the sheep.

9

A New Heart

(Ezekiel 36)

Humans possess a great deal of responsibility for the care of the world. At times, this responsibility can become overwhelming. Faced with the immensity of the tasks before us, we can waver in fear and fail to perform at our best. The extent of God's expectations and goals is frightening! If we do not recognize how intimidating Yahweh's plans are for us, perhaps we have not seen the scope of what God desires for us in the world. It is an enormous task, and our responsibility to work with God in the care of the world is almost beyond belief.

When Ezekiel emphasizes responsibility, the prophet presents a problem. Life with God is more than duty, obligation, and responsibility. What about grace, mercy, creation, and all the other ways in which we talk about God's initiative in reaching people? An emphasis on responsibility can easily develop into an overemphasis, distorting the theological views that Ezekiel also presents. But in Ezekiel 36, the prophet presents an emphasis on God's role in our salvation. God's activity does not deny or contradict human responsibility, but adds to it and transforms it by completing it. Responsibility does not bring salvation to anyone. God saves people for very specific reasons and through specific actions, including the giving of a new heart.

Being Overly Responsible

Ezekiel knows that all of this responsibility is an awesome task and that humans are limited creatures. Moreover, Ezekiel has witnessed repeated exhibitions of the worst of human nature. The prophet has little reason to believe in human reliability, yet he has continually spoken about the need for human responsibility.

We first encountered Ezekiel's notions of responsibility in Ezekiel 18's discussion of morality and individual responsibility. Each person would be held accountable for that one's sins, not for the sins of the previous generation. In this way, each person was responsible for the maintenance of morality and for the construction of the moral community. Though humans did not need to be responsible for the actions of the past, they faced the enormous responsibility of controlling their own actions, and thus for constructing the kind of world that could be morally responsible for itself. In specific terms, Ezekiel 18 taught us about our own responsibility to worship God and to care for each other's well-being. These are immense responsibilities.

In our discussion of Ezekiel 23's story of the two sisters, Oholah and Oholibah, we found a responsibility that was far too intense for any comfort. Instead, we heard in that story a plea that responsibility and punishment need not be identical. Yahweh gives responsibility so that we can participate in God's work of caring for creation, not so that we can be tested and found failing.[1] God is responsible, and invites us to share in that responsibility.

In Ezekiel 34, the prophet's metaphors included sheep and shepherds. The sheep were responsible for caring for the pasture and for helping other to receive a full share of the food; the shepherds were responsible for joining God in the work of caring for the sheep. All needed to make sure that there was enough food and water for all people. Human responsibility means participating in God's work and holding God's values and goals as one's own. Even humans cannot perform the tasks for which they are responsible without God's gifts, because God's partnership in human endeavors makes them possible.

Now, Ezekiel asks more directly a highly pertinent question: how can humans handle this enormous responsibility? Though we have seen the beginnings of answers before, now this concern comes directly to the forefront as Ezekiel discusses how Yahweh will proceed to restore the people. As usual, Ezekiel's thoughts about human responsibility begin with comments about the nature of God. The prophet thus undertakes an analysis of Yahweh's holiness.[2]

A Concern for Holiness (36:16–21)

Yahweh is a holy God. Throughout the Old Testament, holiness can mean several things, but in Ezekiel, holiness often refers to a separation from uncleanness. There are things that Ezekiel considers truly disgusting, and God's holiness means

---

[1] Cp. the familiar notion in John 3:16–17: "For God loved the world so much that God sent the unique Son, in order that everyone who believes in him might not be destroyed but would have eternal life. For God did not send the Son into the world in order to judge the world, but in order that the world might be saved through him." As always, God's efforts intend to save, even though some humans might interpret those efforts as judgment or testing.

[2] For a complete examination of this topic, see John G. Gammie, *Holiness in Israel* (Overtures to Biblical Theology; Minneapolis, Minnesota: Fortress Press, 1989).

that God cannot stand to associate with those things. Holiness, then, is an extremely strong sense of propriety, in which each part of creation must be in its correct place. This extends throughout the human sphere as well as the relationship between God and people: everything must be in the right place, or else God cannot tolerate it. Holiness and orderliness are thus very similar, in this understanding of holiness.

God perceives disgusting disorderliness in the world. Things are not in their right places, and this provokes God's wrath. One example of disorder is bloodshed (36:18). Human blood belongs *inside* people; shed blood violates the divinely appointed order of the world. This notion of holiness as order is a simple, straightforward way to understand God's purposes.[3] When God witnesses such uncleanness, divine holiness requires God to act, and God's action here takes the form of exile.

God's name is holy, and this motivates God's action. What does it mean that God's name is holy? For one, it means that God's name is in the right place, and for Ezekiel this would refer to the temple or any other place where the people worship God. But it must mean more than that. God's name is holy in an active sense, creating holiness and orderliness wherever it goes. The divine name restores order, putting life back into its correct place. When the exiles said that God's name desired them to be outside their original land, it defiled the holy name,

---

[3] Another example is harder for us to understand: the uncleanness of looking at a menstruating woman (36:17). According to the notion of holiness, in which each part of creation has its place, the correct location for menstruating women (as well as people with certain diseases) is in a special area outside the village (cp. Leviticus 12's impurity laws with the treatment of various areas outside the camp in Leviticus 13:46; 14:39–47; Numbers 5:1–4; 31:19; and Deuteronomy 23:10–13). Ezekiel 36:17 refers to menstruating women *inside* the camp, which violates the divine order. Though this practice is hardly commendable by modern standards, it makes this verse understandable. This also shows one of the problems with this view of holiness as cleanness; the very simplicity of the notion can sometimes mislead those who interpret and apply it. Some circumstances require a more nuanced (and thus complex) understanding of holiness.

because the name always works to put people in their proper place (36:20-21). But God is concerned that the name remain holy, and that requires that order be kept where the name of God is present. Such order necessitates God's action to restore holiness.

For God's Sake (36:22–32)

Because of God's name, there will be restoration for the people. God's holiness requires the restoration of life to its proper order. Ezekiel is quite clear about the reasons for this restoration. The prophet charges the people with slander, because they have profaned God's holy name throughout the nations (36:23). In other words, the exiles have falsely blamed God for their troubles, despite the fact that they had brought their destruction upon themselves, and these slanderous accusations have damaged the divine reputation.

God's solution to slander is nothing short of salvation. God will bring all the exiles back together, and will give them back their land (36:24). When this happens, then all the nations of the earth will know that Yahweh is a good and holy God, who is gracious to the chosen people and who keeps everything and everyone—including the Jews—in their proper place. This restoration shows that God is the proper kind of God.[4]

The reason for restoration is clear. The people have not deserved this action; they have not gained their salvation through morality at all. Nor does God save out of mercy, *per se*; that is, salvation comes not because God chooses to overlook the people's failings, nor does it come out of any true sense of kindness or compassion toward the people. Instead, God saves because the divine reputation is at stake. Of course, we can see here the epitome of grace: the reason God saves is precisely that the people do *not* deserve it, because they have defamed God.

---

[4] This reminds the reader of the priestly notion of Exodus, in which God saves the people in order to gain glory for God (Exodus 14:4, 17, 18).

The Removal of the Idols

The beginning of the salvation appears with the removal of idols, for that has been a primary source of uncleanness. The worship of other gods cannot exist within God's chosen people. God shows no desire to remove the idolatry from the whole world, perhaps to replace it with the worship of Yahweh. Instead, God's only concern is the idolatry of the chosen ones. They should not have idols in their midst, but only God. Yahweh is the God of these people, and no other god shall take Yahweh's place. Everything must be in the right place, and that means that Yahweh is in the place of worship and godhood for these people. By removing the idols, God has taken the first step toward the cleansing of these people.

A New Heart

In order to facilitate our involvement in God's great tasks of salvation, God provides each person with a new heart (36:26). This is not a new image for Ezekiel; it appears twice elsewhere in his prophecy. For the prophet, the new heart represents God's salvation (11:19; 18:31). Once the idols are removed, there is still more work to do. God needs active participants in this process, or else the restoration will be useless. If the people have not changed their own intentions and beliefs, what will stop them from repeating the mistakes of the past? For this reason, salvation requires that God give the people new hearts.

There is a very specific purpose for the new heart, as well as the new spirit that God also provides at the same time. Once the people receive this heart of flesh, losing their stony heart, then they can perform God's statutes and ordinances. The result of the new heart is obedience to the Torah, the law of God.[5] With fresh hearts, the people follow God with great energy and vitality, holding fast the requirements of Torah, especially those that speak of holiness, cleanness, and proper

---

[5] In an identical fashion, Jeremiah's new covenant allows renewed compliance with Torah, because it is now written on the people's hearts (Jeremiah 31:31–34).

order. Once the transplantation of hearts is complete, then the people will again contribute to their own social order and will no longer slander or reduce God.

The nature of the new heart is most striking. The heart is made of flesh—hardly a special material. Hearts are supposed to be constructed of flesh! God's new provision is in no way special or rare; in fact, it should be typical for everyone. Thus, the holiness that God requires is also not special in any way; everyone should maintain order and live in holiness. Too easily we think of salvation as changing our nature or making us special, but in Ezekiel's perspective, salvation only makes us what we should have been all along. Salvation is the most natural state; any other condition is strange and temporary. The new heart is the same as the old heart with which we were born. The heart of stone simply did not belong; it violated the divine order, and so God brought us back to where we began.

In the same way, the new heart returns us to the Torah, God's instruction for life. With a new heart, we obey the same old law, as it well should be.[6] God is not fickle, and God's new development in saving the people does not change God's nature. At its roots, salvation is the restoration of the way things were, or at least the ways things should have been. In Ezekiel's day, God's instruction still provided help for daily life in community, just as today God's Torah continues to give guidance for communal life that is moral, peaceful, and compassionate, just as God intends. New hearts do not replace the law or make the law unnecessary in any way. New hearts enable obedience to Torah, and that is exactly the point.

Remembrance

When God's gift of new hearts restores the people and enables once more their adherence to God's law, then salvation occurs. The peace and prosperity that God intends becomes

---

[6] This reminds the Christian reader of Matthew 5:17, in which Jesus declares that his purpose is fulfilling God's Torah, not in removing any part of it.

possible again. There is enough food and resources for all people, and the prosperity amazes them all, as God's people share all their goods among themselves. Once the exiles experience again (or for the first time) the kind of abundant life that God wishes for all people, then they will truly realize deep inside themselves what they have done. After they partake of the divine order, they will admit the desecrations of disorder that they have committed. This is the last step in their restoration, in which they become new people by realizing their own faults and sins and pledging their lives to maintaining the divine order.[7]

For God's Sake

Once again, Ezekiel emphasizes that the salvation occurs for God's sake. Though the people benefit from their restoration in many observable ways, God has not done it for their sake. God does not reward sin and uncleanness; that kind of divine action would be improper and would violate the proper order of life. But God's own nature requires a saved, restored people, and so the extension of salvation is inevitable. Once the people are saved, then they change internally and receive the rewards of the good life that they deserve. All of this occurs for God's sake, because of who God is, and not because of what we have done.

Cleansing and Rebuilding (36:33–36)

In this passage Yahweh makes clear the connection between sin and restoration: "On the day when I make you clean from all your iniquities, I will cause the cities to have inhabitants, and the empty places shall be rebuilt" (36:33). Removing sin and restoring the people are virtually the same task for God; they happen on the same day. People who have been cleansed rebuild; people in a rebuilt society are clean. It works

---

[7] This is a very different understanding of God's salvation than most recent Christian formulations. For Ezekiel, repentance comes *last*, after the people's actions have already changed.

both ways, because of what it means to be clean and holy. Holiness means knowing one's place, and the correct place for God's people requires involvement in the construction of a caring and compassionate society.

The whole world comments that the destroyed places are now like the Garden of Eden, like paradise, because of what God has done (36:35). The restoration was for God's sake, and so it is to God's credit. The goal of this amazing salvation was the restoration of God's reputation throughout the world, and God's action accomplished this. This concern with God's reputation provides a striking contrast to generations such as ours, when we often concentrate more on the church's reputation than on the way the world comes to know God.

There are concrete results to God's restoration. This is not only a spiritual rebirth, but a renewal that allows the people to rebuild. Of course, the extensive rebuilding means that there is a great deal of work for everyone. Ezekiel never claims that God does the work of rebuilding alone; God works with humans as God's partners in shaping the proper, holy society. The construction of this society requires two kinds of work: the rebuilding of the city and reconstitution of the social connections between the people. Both necessitate the vigorous effort of the people. The community's sweat will construct the buildings, and their thoughtful sensitivity will revitalize the morality and the compassion of their human relationships. When the people finish all of this work, then there will be a society worth having, and it will be the place that restores God's reputation among the nations.

Once more, Ezekiel turns the hierarchies of the established religious sensibilities completely around. God provides shocking newness to the people and to the land; together they are God's new servants. No longer can leaders emphasize their domination of others, because they cannot take credit for what they build. No longer can the most moral persons of the community claim that their religious insight maintains the city, because all the people must join together in producing God's desired settlement. All of this is for God's glory. Salvation, then, is for a purpose. Salvation is so that we can live responsible lives in partnership with God.

Increasing the Flock (36:37–38)

With a few final verses, Ezekiel closes off this passage. God offers to fulfill one of the people's wishes: repopulation. They want to be numerous again. The exiles represented perhaps 5 or 10 percent of the previous inhabitants of Jerusalem and Judah. They were a small group, and they wanted to regain their former size, as a first step toward realizing their potential in the world. Perhaps this wish was selfish; they thought of size as a stepping-stone to power and prestige, thinking that biggest would certainly be best. God, however, agreed for different reasons.

In a strange image, God explains the reasons for the salvation that the exiles will experience: it is to increase people like flocks for sacrifice. In that way, the people will know that Yahweh is God. Once more, the prophet emphasizes—in shocking, surprising language—that human salvation occurs for God's sake and for God's purposes. Sacrifice is one of the priestly devices for removing sin from the world. Through sacrifice, God and people join together to deal with sin. In like fashion, our salvation is so that sin is removed from the world, by our action in partnership with God. Yahweh desires a truly restored world, in which sin is no longer present.

God's New World

God bravely desires a new world. In this new world, all people know that Yahweh is God. All sin has been taken away from the world. God's reputation is intact and well known. The old devastations have been swept away and new constructions replace them. The communities of God are vibrant relationships that embody morality and that enjoy peace and prosperity through care and compassion. God's dreams are nothing less than this wonderful vision of a radically changed and redeemed world.

The transformation of the world occurs through an inner change within humans: we receive a new heart and a new spirit. The new heart energizes the change and enables us to do what humans should do: care for each other and experience peace and prosperity. The new heart leads to restoration and salvation, and then to life in a brand new world that makes living easy, because the people in it care for each other, and each has enough for a good life. Then, at the crucial moment of remembering their old life and considering the blessings of new life that they have received from God, the people repent, and complete the inner changes brought about by the new heart.

This new heart is part of God's amazing acts of salvation and cleansing, which God provides indiscriminately to all the people. Salvation is never for those who deserve it, since none deserve it. Instead, salvation comes precisely to those who do not deserve God's attention. This is greatly to God's credit; this is the reputation that God strives to establish throughout the world. Our response is gratitude, but also amazement. We stand in God's presence astonished at the surprising revelations that grace and blessing precede repentance and that God's salvation is purely selfish and thoroughly unmotivated. Once more, God surprises us with gifts we never deserve—and the new heart within us so that, someday, we will deserve what we already have, and then we will proclaim God's wonders throughout God's new world!

10

Them Bones, Them Bones

(Ezekiel 37)

Perhaps only two stories in all the book of Ezekiel have wide familiarity. The first one is the story of Ezekiel's inaugural vision, when the prophet saw wheels within wheels. The song that says "Ezekiel saw the wheel, and the wheel went round and round" has popularized this story. The other familiar passage from the book of Ezekiel is in Ezekiel 37, and it too has found its way into the church's musical heritage: "them bones, them bones." Bones connect themselves to other bones for verse after verse, as people hear the word of the Lord.

The songs remind us of the stories, but the stories themselves are much more complex. Both of these prophetic passages verge on allegories, but we should consider them reports of visions. Ezekiel tells stories of seeing strange things. He strives to put visions into words so that he can share an experience and its meaning with others. As always, putting unique events into common vocabulary proves difficult, but there are enough words here to ignite the imaginations of the readers. Though the vision of the fiery chariot racing through the sky (Ezekiel 1) certainly seems the stranger, more incredible tale to us moderns, Ezekiel seems more astonished by the vision of the dry bones. Perhaps this prophet has grown to expect God to do odd things, and now, whenever God approaches, Ezekiel is wary, expecting God to surprise him. In this story, such expectations are not at all disappointed.

A Trick Question (37:1–3)

This reported vision starts with a trick question. Ezekiel realizes the trick; he's been working with God long enough to recognize such things and to steer clear of them. God's ability to surprise surpasses any human ability to anticipate what God might do next, let alone to predict or control God's action. Ezekiel knows that he must submit and let God do what God wishes, but the reader can sense a bit of reluctance in the prophet's actions. However, Ezekiel can never avoid God, and so the story begins.

God's hand reaches down and sweeps Ezekiel off his feet. Through the air the prophet flies, moved by Yahweh's spirit. Whether this represents a vision that the prophet sees in his own mind or a supernatural place to which God takes the prophet through supernatural means is certainly not the point of this story.[1] As the story goes, God takes Ezekiel away without warning, without even a word to prepare the prophet for this trip. Suddenly, the spirit takes the prophet away, and Ezekiel has no choice and no control.

Once he lands and his vision clears, Ezekiel sees a valley with nothing but old bones. Then God takes Ezekiel on a tour; together they walk through the valley, inspecting the bones piled on the valley floor. The sheer number of the bones

---

[1] Compare Paul's discussion in 2 Corinthians 12:1–5, in which it is not important if such visions of other places occur in the body or not.

amazes Ezekiel; they are nearly beyond comprehension. He also notices how dry these bones are. They are not the bones of the freshly dead. These bones have been exposed to the elements for years. The sun has bleached them, animals have gnawed at the meat and marrow, the winds and flash-floods have scattered them and rearranged them into meaningless patterns. Resuscitations occurred from time to time in the Old Testament narratives, but only to persons who had been dead just a very short time, so short that one might think that the death was only apparent.[2] But no life is possible once the bones are broken, scattered, chewed, and dry. Dry bones are good for nothing.

For Ezekiel, the problem is even worse than that. His earliest training was that of a priest. He knew God's Torah, the law that instructed the people how to live properly and maintain holiness. According to Numbers 19:16, anyone who touched a human bone would be unclean. Here was Ezekiel, surrounded by human bones by the thousands! Faced with such a valley, his first inclination would be to turn the other way and run. Getting closer to the bones would mean that he risked uncleanness and unholiness. But now God had brought Ezekiel to this disgusting place, and even taken him by the hand to lead him through the midst of these vile bones. When Ezekiel would lose his footing for even an instant, he might step on the dry bones and listen to them crackle under his feet. Had it not been God who had brought him into the midst of this evidence of massive death, Ezekiel would have felt that this was the most impure time of his life. Perhaps he still thought so. Certainly, God was surprising!

Ezekiel was thoroughly disturbed by this point in time. The presence of such unclean death threatened his traditional values, but God brought him to that place, and there was no way out. Then God asked a question: "Can these bones live?"

---

[2] See Jon L. Berquist, *Ancient Wine, New Wineskins: The Lord's Supper in Old Testament Perspective* (St. Louis, Missouri: Chalice Press, 1991), chapter 10.

What a ridiculous question! Of course they could not live. Bones are dead; they embody death and can even pass along their uncleanness to thoughtless persons who walk by them, such as Ezekiel. Bones can't live; they're dead. It's obvious. Furthermore, these bones had been dead for a long time. These were not warm corpses, nor were they even properly buried bodies. Perhaps God could have worked some sort of miracle with a whole body, but certainly not with these heaps of dry bones that did not even form complete skeletons.

Ezekiel hardly knew what to think. Could these bones live? Of course they couldn't. It was a law of nature, and there had never been so great a miracle as to revive dry bones. But Ezekiel realized how surprising God could be, and the prophet thought twice before contradicting God. He knew that it was a trick question. Bones could not live, but God was—and is—surprising. So Ezekiel avoided the question, and answered, "Lord Yahweh, you know." Don't ask me, God; only you know what you're going to do this time. The evasive answer worked. *God knew* that only God could know, but God wanted everyone else to know that; that's the whole point of this passage and of much of the rest of Ezekiel. God then began to explain it all to Ezekiel, and the truth of the matter became quite surprising.

These Bones Shall Live (37:4–10)

In the midst of this macabre valley, God told the prophet to do the absurd. Ezekiel was supposed to prophesy to these inanimate bones and to deliver them a message: "I will lead *ru'ach* into you, and you will live" (37:5). This sentence is difficult to understand because of the ambiguity of the Hebrew word *ru'ach*, which can be translated as "wind," "breath," or "spirit."[3] This produces three possible readings for the sentence, and all of them make sense. Quite possibly, this is a type

---

[3] This word, *ru'ach*, is also important in the vision of Ezekiel 1. See chapter 2.

of pun, in which more than one meaning is intended at once. Certainly, each of the three possibilities is instructive.

One possibility is that *ru'ach* here means wind: "I will make the wind to blow through you bones, and you will live." The picture is visually spectacular. The valley floor lies crusted with piles of bones, thrown randomly by the winds of the past, and yet now comes Yahweh's wind, and it roars through the valley. As the intensity of the wind increases, the bones begin to wiggle and writhe with the force, and as the wind approaches the ferocity of a tornado, the bones take leave of the earth and fly through the air. One expects that they will be scattered throughout the valley, smashed against the rocks, and broken into pieces. But no! The bones fly through the air propelled by the great wind, and all of a sudden, two bones collide in midair. When they hit, they do not break, nor do they bounce off each other; they stick together. Soon another bone hits and sticks, and then another. After two hundred and more collisions of bones, a complete skeleton appears, and soon it grows sinews and meat and skin. The image is certainly worthy of today's movies' special effects; one can see it in the mind and be amazed at the image. This seems to coincide with Ezekiel's statement that he heard a rattling, and then the bones came together, bone by bone (37:7).

The second possible reading is "I will breathe my breath into you, and you will live." The reader thinks back to the creation story, and especially to Genesis 2:7, when Yahweh forms an earthling from the dust and mud, and then bends down over the creature and breathes breath into its nostrils, giving it life. Through the same means, God breathes the breath of life into these bones, which then fly together of their own accord to form skeletons, with sinews and muscles and tissue and flesh growing spontaneously. In this vision, God creates the new Israel in much the same way that God created the first humans, though the materials are different. God's care appears clearly in this image, as God once more stoops to the ground to bring life to humanity. The first reading was spectacular; this reading is much more tender. God's breath means

life. Also, by this interpretation, God willfully touches these
bones, violating the laws of cleanness and in that fashion
breaking the boundary of death. God's breathing breath into
the reconstituted corpses required closeness and contact with
death. Death spoiled cleanness and rendered unholy anything
it touched, but in this understanding God seeks out the unclean things and makes them clean, giving them life itself.

A third possible nuance also arises for consideration. The
sentence can be translated, "I will lead spirit into you, and you
will live." In this sense, we readers can clearly understand that
God's spirit brings life. This passage then comes close to
incarnation, because God places spirit into human bodies,
which then become alive. The bodies are receptacles for the
spirit that God places therein. Though it is not God who
inhabits these bodies, perhaps it is not clear that these are
human spirits, either. God seems involved in some radically
new kind of creation, the likes of which the world has never
before seen.

Ezekiel delivers the saying about the *ru'ach*, and he prophesies this to the bones, and life enters them. Together, the new
people made out of these bones stand in their places, and they
form a very large army, ready—but ready for what?

Up from the Grave (37:11–14)

This one of Ezekiel's visions is exceedingly strange; it
stretches the bounds of what humans can imagine. Yahweh
then explains to the prophet what all of this is supposed to
mean; the vision becomes allegorical. The bones correspond to
the exiles from Jerusalem, who lament that their loss is as great
as death. Yahweh sends a message to these mourning exiles: "I
am opening your graves and I will raise you up from your
graves, O my people, and I will bring you to the land of Israel"
(37:12). Exile is death, and God grants them the resurrection
of returning to their ancestral homeland.

The chief point of this vision is that God promises the
exiles a restoration to Jerusalem. Ezekiel's prophecies have

shifted from his earliest messages because he now observes a new historical situation and envisions a different future. At the start of his prophecy, he argued against any possibility for the repopulation of Jerusalem, because the full defeat of Jerusalem had not yet happened. Ezekiel 37 must come later, well after Babylonia had accomplished the full destruction of Judah. At this later time, Ezekiel offers a word of encouragement, suggesting that God will someday provide them with restoration. The timing is left quite vague, however. No one knows the day, but God will save the people.

The statement about *ru'ach* is rephrased here: "I will put my *ru'ach* in you and you will live" (37:14). Though most translations offer "spirit" as a translation, "breath" is also possible. Infused with this *ru'ach*, the people live, and God places them in Jerusalem and Judah.

The story of the dry bones ends with God's statement that the people will thus know that Yahweh has spoken these things and has done them. Again, the proper knowledge of Yahweh is vital. When God asked Ezekiel the trick question at the opening of the story, Ezekiel answered, "Lord Yahweh, you know." Knowledge rightly belongs to God, not to any other. Who knows the extent to which God will go to surprise the people? Ezekiel doesn't know, and neither do any of the rest of us. But God knows, and God wishes that we have that knowledge, too. Bit by bit, story by story, we gain the knowledge of who God is, and that knowledge never ceases to amaze and surprise.

Part of God's nature fights death, yet to speak of this chapter as "victory over death" overinterprets the passage itself. First of all, this is a vision, not an actual event. Ezekiel sees these things in a supernatural experience of a dream or vision, and then he reports it to the exiles. There are other reasons, as well. There is no struggle between God and death, so there is hardly any sense that God is victorious over vicious Death. Death will continue, to be sure; there is no hint at all that Ezekiel would not die, or that this revived and resuscitated army would escape a second death. Victory happens, nonetheless. Unlike other prophecies of Ezekiel, the motivation for

God's action does not jump to the forefront, but it is there nonetheless. God desires knowledge.

This works in two ways. First, God desires that we know God's nature. From this vision and its report, we should learn God's concern for restoring the people. Also, we can learn the importance of spirit in the midst of our lives and God's willingness to bring together disparate factions and pieces of persons and communities. Second, God calls us into a close, intimate relationship, in which we know God. For this relationship to happen, people must be alive. God works to bring people to life as a first step toward that relationship. Life itself seems of little importance, even in this miraculous vision. Relationship with God is the truly important thing, which life makes possible. God's gift of spirit also enables this relationship, for it seems to create a special linkage between God and people. Just as God gives people new spirits along with new hearts (36:26), the infusion of God's spirit empowers a new condition of life. Having received new spirits and having observed how God enlivens people, we understand God's nature all the better, and we enter into the close intimacy with God that is called knowledge.

The Body of God's People

In the vision of the dry bones, God creates new bodies out of scattered skeletons and forms a living army, a new organization or body of persons.[4] Victory over individual death seems a minor issue in this vision, when compared to the creation of this larger body, which is built for God's purposes. The new body of God's people is the point of overlap between the vision and the prophetic explanation—God desires a new body of people.

---

[4] One of this vision's spooky, haunting features is this massive army (37:11). They assemble in the valley with hardly a signal or a sound, appearing as if they are ready to march off into battle against an enormous foe. But the vision fades then, and the reader never knows the purpose or outcome of the army. It remains a mystery, as does much in the book of Ezekiel.

The parallels between this notion and Paul's idea of the body of Christ is clear (1 Corinthians 12:12–31).[5] When Paul wants to describe the unity and diversity of God's new people, the choice of a body metaphor seems obvious. Human bodies consist of numerous parts that seem quite different; Paul lists eyes, ears, head, and feet. These parts do not look like each other at all, and each functions in a very distinct way, yet all of them are typical parts of human bodies. Though different people have different parts, and though the human body can function well without certain parts, no single-cell creature is human. Humanity requires the integration of difference on a physical level. That is the value of this metaphor, whether we examine Ezekiel's development of the idea or Paul's usage of this theme. The body of Christ and the dry bones revived both point to the fact that God's people have diverse personalities and persons.

To push this point, surely both the prophet and the apostle recognize the vitality of diversity and the danger of uniformity. Diversity defines God's people; there is no such thing as a uniform life of faith or a single type of believer. The extent of God's family is far too broad for that; those who work toward uniformity damage that family through their single-minded insistence on sameness. Uniformity brings death. This is the subject of Paul's use of the body of Christ metaphor; without the diversity of gifts and persons, there can be no church. The dry bones in Ezekiel's vision offer a wonderful description of this, as well. These bones represent persons who once experienced life in all its fullness and all its diversity, but now they have been reduced to sameness. No one can tell one person's bones from anyone else's. As weather and time have broken the bones into pieces, distinguishing leg bones, for instance, from any others becomes increasingly difficult. The scattered, smashed bones symbolize perfect uniformity, but the bones also show the deathliness of sameness.

Of course, diversity is only one necessary element within God's body. God requires that unity harness the diversity for

---

[5] Paul also uses this metaphor in Ephesians 3:6, 4:12.

God's purposes. Unity itself can never be the goal, nor should believers think that diversity itself is the end. Unity and diversity are both necessary, but they are necessary means to an end—the performance of God's will. Diversity provides the energy and vitality, because of the variety of gifts, skills, perspectives, and opinions that combine with amazing power. Unity focuses this diversity, steering the sheer power of diversity into God's direction. God's purposes provide the goal for both unity and diversity.

This passage challenges the reader with one other issue. From what does God build the new body in Ezekiel 37? God constructs the people from dead things, which the law itself condemns as unclean. The people of God originate in the most deathly substance of the world. In the reviving of these bones, there is no repentance, nor is there any willful decision or belief. The bones live because God desires, not at all because the people deserve it. This is grace in its purest form, transforming death itself into life. If the dead become God's chosen ones, how much more can others considered unclean become God's people? If even the dead receive the spirit before any repentance or works or choice of appropriate lifestyle, how much more so does God's spirit pervade the living people of today without requiring them to change to meet churchly standards? God's spirit in Ezekiel 37 violates the limits of the law, even the law that God had pronounced, and in the same way God's spirit continues to overstep the boundaries of human propriety and even the limits of divine prerogative. God surprises us once more with a willingness to go to any lengths to bring life, even to those we think undeserving or undesirable, even to those whom Yahweh had condemned to death. In that valley God does unexpected things that shock, that amaze, and that instruct about God's true nature and desire that all should live in the people of God.

The Sign-act of the Sticks (37:15–28)

A sign-act follows this amazing vision of the dry bones' revival. On Yahweh's command, Ezekiel takes two sticks in his hands and writes on them. The first stick represents the northern kingdom of Israel, which had been dead for more than a century by this time. The other stick stands for Judah, the death of which was recent and painfully close. Ezekiel brings the two sticks together and holds them in one hand, symbolizing that God desires the unity of the two nations that had been so long divided, and that God commits to bringing the two together. As Ezekiel explains the sign-act, he affirms God's covenanting to restore both the nations as a unity, made out of the diversity.

Ezekiel uses the prophetic words following this simple sign-act to unite three of the themes on which he has recently focused. Ezekiel 34 discusses leadership with the metaphor of shepherdry; Ezekiel 36 focuses on restoration and the unity of the people in their homeland with new hearts and new spirits; and Ezekiel 37:1–14 describes God's desire for unity and diversity in the newly revived people. Now, Ezekiel brings these thoughts together into one unified statement with diverse nuances, forming a clear statement of Ezekiel's restorative thought.

The first themes that enter discuss the shepherding of the people. God's servant David will lead them all. There will be no king, only a shepherd, the most humble of guides. David will lead all the people, both from Israel and from Judah, together as simple folk in their old ancestral homeland. Together, there will be a covenant of peace between God and the whole people. This peace will show both the end of hostilities and the beginning of true relationships and of sufficient resources for all. The ideas of return to the homelands repeat the themes of restoration (36:8–12; cp. 37:25). Then, Ezekiel announces that God's dwelling place will be in the midst of the people, suggesting the same process as that by which God's spirit inhabited and animated the dry bones.[6]

Again, the motivation for this restoration is the knowledge of the nations. All the world must know that Yahweh is God,

---

[6] This theme also appears at the very end of the book of Ezekiel (48:35b).

and they must recognize God's nature by observing the life of God's people. The people are unwitting worldwide witnesses to God's very being, simply by living their lives as restored persons in God's new land. For this reason, grace has brought them restoration, but there is also responsibility, because God expects the right kind of witness. But in this passage another notion enters; God also desires a sanctuary in the midst of the sanctified people. Worship joins the themes that Ezekiel combines here, in a passage that functions to unify the diversity of themes presented throughout the book.[7]

Togetherness and Restoration

Unity and togetherness are problems for Ezekiel's period of history, and thus the prophet addresses these issues. Ezekiel watches the dissipation of his people. They enter unwillingly into their diaspora and are scattered throughout the world. The prophet addresses his companions in Babylonian exile with a message that God desires all of them to be together once more. Diaspora provides the energy and the diversity that will drive the next generation of God's people, but the unity of purpose is necessary. Through new hearts and also through the presence of God's reviving spirit, Yahweh creates a new people out of dry bones that seem to offer no hope at all for the future.

The message for today seems little changed. God's people now require different parts of the body, different types of people for the fulfillment of God's purposes. Our own society possesses its own diasporas, including all the persons whom we have shut out of our lives, our circle of friends, our churches, our cities, our nation, our leadership, our ministry, and every other part of life that we try to control. These many diasporas of shunned and scattered people will provide the energy for the future of our faith, if only we can embrace them in their radical

---

[7] Ezekiel 37:24–28 functions so well as a summary of Ezekiel 1—37 that it may well have been the original end to an early version of the book of Ezekiel.

and perhaps disturbing difference and join our life with them. God offers the surprising example of embracing what is unlawful, what is deathly, and what is unclean in order to bring life; we can settle for no less ourselves.

Out of death, God brings life; out of our broken lives, God brings unity. Once more, the unity of salvation comes for a purpose: to serve as God's servants in the world. God saves the backsliders and the defiled ones, the destroyed and dishonored, the unrespected and lost, bringing them all together into God's own people. Once assembled, God places them in the middle of the world, to serve as a sanctuary for all nations to see God's glory. When God's people are restored, then the world will flock to them because God's people make God's mission seem so attractive.

This also provides for us a new vision of the church. The church must consist of the broken and deathly things of the world. It is not enough to say that the church must admit the rejected ones; the rejected ones must make up the church and must truly be the church. Through God's salvation, these wildly disparate parts come together and receive new life, but only once they are together. As separate bones, there can be no life; as reconstituted bodies that accept difference, new life suddenly, surprisingly arrives unbidden. This life drives them forward to a new role within the world, fulfilling God's purpose of a witness to the nations. Such must be today's church.

11

Gog of Magog

(Ezekiel 38—39)

What happens next?
That's a popular question in our time, as it is in many cultures throughout the history of the world. Sometimes our efforts to know the future before it arrives result in boring, technical information, such as that produced by economists and government bureaucrats. If we know that the next fiscal year's real inflation-adjusted growth in the Gross Domestic Product will be 1.2%, that knowledge may affect our planning, but it's hardly an exciting revelation for most people. At other times, our efforts to predict the future become trivialized to the point of being lightweight entertainment, such as when the newspapers in the grocery-store checkout line predict that next year a certain movie star will shave off all hair and move into a religious sect in India. But from time to time, our fascination with the future attaches itself to more important, life-and-

death issues, and in some of these cases it seems that cataclysmic events will soon overtake the normalcy of our lives and replace it with radically different conditions that will be almost unrecognizable.

In recent decades, the United States has experienced a renewed interest in things called, rightly or wrongly, eschatology and apocalypticism. Eschatology is the knowledge of the end-times, either the end of the present era or the end of the world. Eschatological speculation assumes that there will be some sudden change in the way the world works, and that it will come soon, certainly within the lifetime of those studying the end. When scientists predict how many billion years it will take for the sun to increase its heat to the point where life on earth becomes impossible, this is not typical eschatology, in part because the predicted cataclysm will not happen in our lifetimes. This kind of speculation provides interesting academic discussion and scientific investigation, but it never captures the popular attention, because it is all too far away. But when one preacher predicts that the world will end on a certain date next October, it becomes a national media event, because people want to know what the future holds, especially if the near future will experience a sudden, severe change from anything previously known. That is eschatology.

Apocalyptic literally refers to "hidden things." The term refers to religious ideas that assume that there is some sort of hidden knowledge that will enable someone to know special things, especially things about the supernatural world.[1] Often, this knowledge has come to all people, but only those with the special insight can interpret the knowledge in the proper way. For the most recent apocalyptic movements, this means that the Bible contains certain passages that, if interpreted with the right insights, will reveal important details of the future. All the pertinent facts are present, but most people will never

---

[1] See John J. Collins, "Apocalyptic Literature," in *Harper's Bible Dictionary*, ed. Paul J. Achtemeier (San Francisco: Harper & Row, 1985), pp. 35–36.

know the code that unlocks the secrets of antiquity from pages of the sacred book. This would mean that God revealed things about the future in scripture, but that these revelations were shielded, so that some of the essential knowledge became hidden. In medieval times it was sometimes thought that the conversion of the Bible's letters into numbers would allow a manipulation of the text and a revelation of a hidden meaning behind the plain sense of the biblical text. Apocalypticism searches for those hidden passages and finds its truth therein. The results of such apocalyptic movements are evident; incidents such as the Branch Davidian group's battle against the government of the United States take over our newspaper headlines and seize the popular imagination for months.

The most recent apocalyptic movements have seized upon certain statements in the Bible, using various codes to unlock the meaning that they assume hidden there. Once-popular methods such as numerology are rarely employed any more, but other schemes are much more prevalent. Certain biblical books present themselves for this apocalyptic speculation, because those books represent the products of ancient apocalyptic thought. Ancient religious writers tried to unlock the secrets of the future, and they recorded their speculations. Biblical apocalyptic depended upon strange words that probably parodied more well-known figures or echoed names from the distant past. It also made heavy use of periodizations of history, which interpreted all world history as a small number of stages, each representing a distinct age or era. Usually, biblical apocalyptic writers understood themselves to live at the end of one of the later eras, and they expected cataclysmic change within a matter of years. The apocalyptic of the Bible includes the books of Daniel and Revelation, and also parts of books such as Ezekiel and Mark.

Ezekiel 38—39 tells the story of Gog, a king from a land called Magog, who is the chief prince of Meshech and Tubal.[2]

---

[2] Often in recent popularizing literature, Gog and Magog have been misunderstood as the names of two individuals or of two nations.

These lands are unknown within biblical and ancient history, and no attempt to locate these places or to explain them has ever been successful, though they seem to be in Asia Minor.[3] The time span of transmission has lost Ezekiel's original apocalyptic code and no amount of effort now can possibly recover it. The prophecy directed toward Gog takes on allegorical tones; Ezekiel apparently wants to tell us about something more than a historical nation. These two chapters also appear similar to the oracles against the nations. Certainly there are many statements that are similar to words from the denunciation of Egypt and Tyre in Ezekiel 25—32, but there are also great differences. Egypt and Tyre were historical realities, and Ezekiel predicted (both rightly and wrongly) what historical and political events would befall these regions in the coming years. With regard to Gog, there is a consistent feel of a non-historical situation. The prophecy is too stylized to represent mere temporal politics; Ezekiel here points to a reality that transcends the bounds of history.

Apocalyptic Eschatology

Apocalyptic and *eschatology* are both unfamiliar terms, and so it can be helpful to discuss them at greater length. Both of them deal with time and interpretation. Eschatology focuses on the end-times and offers predictions about what will happen then, often based on the realities of the present and the history of the past. Apocalyptic interprets events surrounding the community all throughout the past, present, and future.

Wondering About the Future

Apocalyptic eschatology takes the form of speculation about the future. What will happen next? Will our nation still be around in ten years? Will some other power conquer us? Will the economy be good? Will our faith survive? This wondering

---

[3] See John G. Gammie, "Meshech," in *Harper's Bible Dictionary*, ed. Paul J. Achtemeier (San Francisco: Harper & Row, 1985), p. 629.

about the future leads to answers expressed in the form of apocalyptic.

For Ezekiel, the shocking, destabilizing experience of exile prompted this speculation about the future. Would the next years have the same uproar of the last decade? Would exile last?

In our own time, uncertainty about the future gives rise to apocalyptic thinking. Maybe we are at the end of time, and soon things will change drastically when God steps into the world to take control. Once this possibility roots itself in the mind, then apocalyptic eschatological suggestions begin. Perhaps God will come soon, dropping down through the clouds to rescue us and take us away. Perhaps another country will soon attack us, trying to destroy us with nuclear weapons. Perhaps we will soon arise and take the place that is rightfully ours. Perhaps we can soon vanquish our religious foes, showing all the world that ours is the only true God. Perhaps we will all die in a fiery inferno when our enemies overtake us. Perhaps one certain situation will happen soon, perhaps another kind of event will soon come to pass. The speculation grows, but then decisions have to be made. The community must determine which of these possible futures it believes. To do this, they begin a search for some other information.

Reinterpreting the Past

Some of that necessary information can come from an analysis of the past. How has history worked before? If we can answer that, then perhaps we can figure out what will happen next. This requires a sharp understanding of the previous years and maybe even the previous centuries. Historical knowledge is needed, but so is insight. Usually, this insight relates to some present event. In our century, much apocalyptic speculation has revolved around key historical events, such as the rise and fall of Germany's Third Reich and the mid-century growth of the United States of America and the former Union of Soviet Socialist Republics as dominant "superpowers." Because of the grand scope of these historical occurrences, they have attracted speculation and formed the insights used to organize the past in apocalyptic interpretations. These interpretations inquire about the roots of such events and use them as guiding principles to understand history. Thus, apocalyptic combines contemporary insights with past data to form a new interpretation of history that strives to explain the present and then the future.

In Ezekiel's time, the primary historical event of importance to the Jews was the Babylonian conquest and subsequent exile. The experience of exile also caused a re-evaluation of the past, as has been seen at several points throughout the book of Ezekiel. What went wrong? Why did the exile happen? Did we deserve defeat? These questions fermented the nascent apocalypticism of Ezekiel's time. The people began to interpret their history in terms of whether they deserved punishment. In particular, they blamed the political leaders, especially the kings, for doing the evil that angered God and created the conquest and exile. Following this interpretation of history, the people deduced that living righteous lives would allow them to escape future punitive action from God, but that sin endangered their earthly, political existence. They knew that the human tendency to sin was great, and so their hopes were slight. But still they strove to speculate about a future that would give them opportunity to live as they desired.

An Agenda for the Present

Perhaps the primary impetus for apocalyptic eschatology is the desire to know what to do in the present. Though apocalyptic describes the future and interprets the past as somehow consistent with the future, it also provides clues about how to live life in the here-and-now. A clear example occurs when some modern-day apocalyptic group concludes that the end of the world will come in just a few months, and then the whole group sells their belongings and moves together into communal life. They make these decisions based upon their view of the world's future; apocalyptic determines present actions, often for people who are seeking solutions for very short-term situations.

In apocalyptic, it is common to believe that God will soon step into history to take direct charge of world affairs. This implies a belief that God and God's people are not now in control, or at least are not able to determine all events. Evil forces rule the world, but soon God will conquer them. In such thinking, the people who write the apocalyptic feel out of control. Without the ability to shape the world in the direction they would like, they wonder what to do in the present. If they were able to change things themselves and to create by their own energies a better world, perhaps they would not be apocalyptic. Their helplessness and their deep sense of futility stimulate their apocalyptic thinking. Soon God will intervene, and even though we are relatively powerless now, we can prepare for God's coming.

Ezekiel 38—39 does not offer a fully developed apocalyptic and eschatological scenario, despite the ways in which modern apocalypticists have interpreted it. Instead, this prophetic story about Gog of the land of Magog offers some limited speculation about what might happen in the future, with the purpose that the hearers and readers of this story might understand their present situation better and make their decisions and perform their activities accordingly. Moreover, Ezekiel's prophecy for Gog reflects on the nature of God, which provides an enduring ground for life for all of God's people.

Gog's Origins (38:1–16)

God commands Ezekiel to prophesy to this king Gog. Yahweh knows that Gog of Magog is assembling a vast army, with numerous northern allies. Amazingly, God is in control of this military expansion, and God even sets a time for battle. It seems that Yahweh supports Gog's militarism and prepares his armies for warfare. The passage sounds as if Yahweh will use Gog for God's own purposes. But then the passage shifts, and God declares that at an appointed time, Gog will rise up against Israel.

Here it becomes clear that Ezekiel is prophesying about a distant future time. By this time, the Jewish exiles in Babylonia have gone back to the ancestral homelands, as Ezekiel had already prophesied that they would. Time passes, and the people restore their full lives (38:14). They rebuild their country that Babylonia had ravished and that had lain in waste for years afterward. However, the Jewish people now live a new kind of life; their villages are unwalled (38:11) because they have replaced their militarism with a reliance upon God. This moves the vision from the futuristic to the counterfactual. The threat from Gog comes long after the threat from Babylonia, well after Israel rebuilt itself into God's special people. Clearly, God's people are idealized, not at all reflecting the historical realities that God's people have constructed over the millennia. But then Gog advances like a storm over the land with speed, strength, and power.[4] Then Yahweh announces the divine intention: God orders the massive, overwhelming armies of Gog to attack Israel. This time God's surprise seems macabre and evil; after restoring the exiles, God again sends an army to destroy them.

Gog's Destruction (38:17—39:20)

Quickly the tables turn. When Gog approaches Israel, his armies are not able to launch the first arrow or make the first slash with the sword. Yahweh attacks the armies of Magog with the very forces of nature; hail and rain drive back the

---

[4] This image echoes the opening image of Yahweh coming over the desert like a storm, emphasizing the fear caused by such an apparition. Perhaps Ezekiel 1—39 once circulated as an independent book, before the addition of Ezekiel 40—48. In such an earlier version of the volume of Ezekiel's prophecies, this image forms a suitable companion to the beginning. In Ezekiel 1 a storm goes from Jerusalem to Mesopotamia; here the storm goes the opposite direction. This storm carries death and destruction; the earlier storm carried God, bringing possibilities for the restoration of life. The latter image is not a reversal of the former, and that becomes the emphasis of Ezekiel 38—39: God now protects Jerusalem and all of Israel from danger.

approaching soldiers (38:22). God never intended to use Gog
to destroy Israel; God intended to demonstrate Israel's safety!
As Yahweh proudly proclaims:

> My holy name will I make known in the midst of my
> people, Israel. I will not allow my holy name to be
> profaned ever again! The nations will know that I am
> Yahweh, the Holy One in Israel.
>
> Ezekiel 39:7

After the enormous defeat of Gog, Israel gathers the weapons and burns them. There is no stockpiling of weaponry;
there is no need for defense. Yahweh has thoroughly destroyed
the armies of Magog and its allies, and the carcasses are food for
the birds. Gog began as the mightiest of the leaders of the
world, and ends in the worst desecration possible. Yahweh's
defense of restored, saved, moral Israel is complete.

Israel's Restoration (39:21–29)

In that day, all the world will witness Israel's salvation, so
that they know God. Though sin caused the exile, God puri-
fied the people and saved them, bringing them back to their
land and making them inviolable. After the debacle of Gog,
Israel can forget its shame and once more hold its head high,
covered in the spirit that Yahweh pours out upon its people.
Yahweh regains the divine reputation and becomes known
worldwide for holiness in Israel. The restoration is truly complete.

The Assurance of the Future

This apocalyptic story offers the exiles an assurance of the
future. They hear this story when they are still impoverished
exiles in Babylonia, with little opportunity to ever regain their
land. Ezekiel not only prophesies that they will someday leave
exile and regain their land, but that once there they will be
inviolate, and all the nations will know that their God is holy

and powerful. After restoration comes continuing protection, and they will never need to face war again.

Perhaps this story comes later in the exile. Ezekiel and others arrived in Babylonia around 597 B.C.E., and other exiles arrived after Jerusalem's fall in 586 B.C.E. Ezekiel had prophesied Jerusalem's destruction and the exiles' hopelessness in those first years, but after Babylonia's conquest was complete, Ezekiel started talking about restoration. Ezekiel was no longer preaching when Cyrus' Persian forces overtook Babylonia and allowed the return of the exiles to their homelands in 539 B.C.E., but Ezekiel may have lived long enough to foresee that a nation, either Persia or some similarly rising power to the north, would someday become as great a threat as Babylonia was in his day. Such might have been possible around 570 B.C.E.[5] Even if there should ever arise a power nearly as great as Babylonia, God will protect the chosen, restored people; they will never again suffer as they did in Ezekiel's day.

Of course, we know that Ezekiel could not envision the sufferings of God's people in the intervening centuries. But Persia did arise, and Persia did not destroy Jerusalem when the opportunity was present, and Ezekiel was correct in that.

Ezekiel's prophecy also critiques any notions of war as fruitless and evil. The safest places in the world are the unwalled villages in the countryside around Jerusalem. Weapons must not be placed in stockpiles, but are good only for burning. Yahweh keeps the people safe; weapons never do. When Babylonia first took exiles in 597 B.C.E., no amount of defense could deter that great power. Though Jerusalem's government courted Egyptian aid in the next decade, this maneuvering resulted only in greater destruction in 586 B.C.E. The message is clear: military attempts to achieve power will fail. In the words of a much later proverb, those who live by the sword, die by the sword. If Israel ever again takes up arms, they violate

---

[5]For the differing prophecies and conditions of the Persian period, see Jon L. Berquist, *In Persia's Shadow: The Beginnings of Second Temple Judah* (Minneapolis, Minnesota: Fortress Press, forthcoming).

this picture of restored life with God, as would any nation that develops weapons and trusts in them. Yahweh is not at all impressed with earthly power, including the military might of Egypt, Israel, Babylonia, Persia, Gog, or any modern nation. In Ezekiel's allegorical story about Gog, it becomes painfully—and graciously—obvious that Yahweh rejects militarism.

Throughout this lengthy allegory, Ezekiel makes his point crystal clear by explaining the goal of all this action. All nations will see God's glory and will admit that Yahweh is God of all. God desires to display holiness, providing an example for the world. These are universalistic visions, albeit in the type of strange language that we have come to expect from Ezekiel. God saves Israel by divine mercy to serve as a beacon to all nations of God's salvation. With a saved, restored Israel at the center of the world, God proceeds to save all people. Ezekiel never considers the ramifications of this early universalist thought, though the final portions of the book of Isaiah certainly reach stunning conclusions about God's will for the whole world.

In this sense Ezekiel 38—39 suddenly becomes an anti-apocalyptic text. The right kind of knowledge about the future is the knowledge of *God*, not the secret knowledge of apocalypticism. The exiles of Ezekiel's day do not require a seer to predict for them the future. They need no secret source of divine information in order to make their decisions in their present times. The Jewish exiles living in ancient Babylonia need the same thing we need: knowledge of God's nature and intimate relationship with Yahweh. These provide the certainty for the present and the assurance for the future that we need for life. No ecstatic visions can ever provide that. In the end, Ezekiel is not an apocalypticist; he is first and always a priest, who finds the present experience of God to be more important than future speculation.

12

A New Temple

(Ezekiel 40—48)

The book of Ezekiel ends where it begins, with a prophetic vision of God's presence. Much has happened since that inaugural vision, however, and so this vision is much different. Ezekiel's upbringing as a priest shows through in both the beginning and ending visions. In Ezekiel 1, the prophet was deeply concerned with God's presence. How could God be with the people now that they lived in a foreign land? How could God break free of the Jerusalem temple and unite with the people elsewhere in the world? The issue of the temple remained in the background of Ezekiel's first vision, when the chariot brought Yahweh into Babylonia. Ezekiel discovered that the temple could not limit God. In this final vision, Yahweh returns to Jerusalem to inhabit not only a new temple, but also the whole nation. God will live in the midst of the newly restored people.

Temples are very important items in religion, especially ancient religion. The construction of a new temple, more than any other single act, would signal the advent of a new era for the people, guaranteeing God's favor and the reality of peace and prosperity. Ezekiel's entire message has shown that this era depends on God's presence with the people. As the message concludes, the prophet emphasizes the newness of the era. This is the restoration of the past grandeur, but more importantly it is the commencement of a new manner of life with God.

The Vision Begins (40:1–4)

When this final vision begins, the narrator tells us readers the date that Ezekiel saw these things. The year was 572 B.C.E. Ezekiel and his compatriots had spent twenty-five years of their lives in exile, in Babylonia near the river Chebar. For the last fourteen of those years, they had lived with the knowledge that Jerusalem had been destroyed and the temple there had been leveled. Ezekiel was probably approaching the age of fifty-five, which for persons of his day was a ripe old age, very near to the end of life. This vision is more than the climax of the book; it is the capping-stone to the great career of a would-be priest turned prophet.[1]

In visions, Ezekiel travels far from Babylonia and alights in Jerusalem. The name of the city itself is never mentioned, but Ezekiel lands on a tall mountain in Israel with a nearby city, and the rest of the vision leaves no doubt that this is Jerusalem, the site of the once and future temple for Yahweh. When Ezekiel reaches this place, he notices an odd man with a measuring stick in hand. This man notices Ezekiel, and tells Ezekiel to listen closely and consider everything that he sees, so

---

[1] Though Ezekiel 40—48 was probably not written by the same prophet Ezekiel who wrote the rest of the book, the narrative of the text allows itself to be understood with this last section as the final vision of the prophet. The narrative flow does not exclude Ezekiel's authorship.

that the prophet can report all of this vision to the exiles, who so need to know about such things. The vision on the banks of the river Chebar seemed almost to have come for the prophet's own personal edification, but this vision is quite the opposite. Ezekiel's mystical guide declaims plainly that the purpose for Ezekiel's presence is the proclamation of these sights to all the exiles. The vision occurs only to empower the prophecy that must follow. In that light, it is strange that the book ends with Ezekiel still in the middle of the seeing. The narrative never follows him back to Babylonia, out of the dream-state of the vision, to the people, where the prophet describes all of what he saw, possibly providing commentary and explanation about the meaning of these visions. Instead, the book leaves its readers with the fresh, powerful ambiguity and uncertainty of the vision itself. We see what the prophet himself sees; even though no one explains it to us we hope that it will be apparent for all to understand.

As in most of the latter portions of the book of Ezekiel, this vision concentrates on a time of the future. In reality the construction of the second Jerusalem temple began more than fifty years after the date of this vision, but Ezekiel may envision a closer time that would still not be immediate.[2] Other events must happen before this vision can come to pass: the migration back to Jerusalem and Judah must have already occurred or at least it must be in progress. Once the people are resettled in Judah, then they can begin to think about rebuilding the temple. Regardless of the exact order in which these events of restoration would occur, Ezekiel's vision in these final chapters should be considered a blueprint for restoration and reconstruction. The prophet provides some concrete plans for the events of the first years back in Judah and for the rebirth of the society of the people who will live there.

---

[2] The story of temple construction can be found in Ezra, Haggai, and Zechariah. See Jon L. Berquist, "Haggai," and "Zechariah," in *Mercer Commentary on the Bible,* ed. Watson E. Mills (Macon, Georgia: Mercer University Press, forthcoming).

A New Temple (40:5—42:20)

Ezekiel provides exhaustive plans for the exact construction of a new temple in Jerusalem. The strangely glowing man whom Ezekiel met at the beginning of this chapter guides the prophet through the vision's already-completed structure, and Ezekiel remembers the dimensions and materials so that he can give those specifications to the exiles, who would one day build that very temple that Ezekiel saw in the vision.

This temple is not the same as the first one, which was built by Solomon almost four hundred years earlier. Ezekiel's temple is somewhat idealized. He seems fascinated by its perfection and symmetry.[3] The more the prophet emphasizes the perfect nature of this new temple, the less it seems that it is a blueprint for the reconstruction of the old, traditional temple. Ezekiel imagines a people who are completely restored and who will then build a temple worthy of their new status to reflect the new and vital things that Yahweh has done for them since the destruction of the old temple. They will not repeat the mistakes of the past, nor will they rebuild the same temple. Instead, the prophet suggests that they build a temple that is perfect in its symmetry, reflecting the perfect relationship that the people now experience with Yahweh.

God Returns (43:1–12)

Once the temple construction reaches its finish, then the next step is the dedication of the temple so that worship can

---

[3] Later theological speculation suggested that there were actually two temples: one in Jerusalem and one in heaven. Ezekiel saw the one in heaven so that the Jerusalem temple could be built as an exact replica. This idea lies behind some of the New Testament book of Hebrews and its theology. Also, the book of Revelation reacts against it when arguing that in the new Jerusalem there is no temple, because God is everywhere throughout the city (Revelation 21:22, but there is a heavenly temple in Revelation 7:15; 11:19; 14:15, 17; 15:5, 6, 8; 16:1, 17). This provides an interesting contrast to Ezekiel's understanding in chapters 40—48, which may seem suddenly before its time.

take place inside. Temples are much, much more than buildings; they are dwelling places for God and locales for the people's worship. Since God is holy, the temple must be made holy, a process that can be termed sanctification or purification. This process necessitates several things. Proper temple worship demands the right kind of human leadership, and it also requires that these proper priests ritually cleanse the furnishings of the temple. The temple should be a pure place, without sin, in order to remove the sins of the world. As important as these elements of the temple purification are to the success of the temple, the truly essential element is the presence of God. Without Yahweh's agreement to live within the temple precincts and to hear the prayers and observe the sacrifices offered there, true worship would be impossible.

Ezekiel's guide leads the prophet to the east gate of the temple court. From that vantage point, he looks off into the distance, and sees a cloud in the east. It looks as if it is the same vision that Ezekiel saw on the banks of the river Chebar to begin his prophetic career; Yahweh comes in a chariot, in the midst of a cloud. But now Yahweh arrives back in Jerusalem from the east, from the same Babylonian exile experienced by the Jewish people. God was with them through their suffering and struggle, and now God is with them in their restoration.

As the cloud of God's glory approaches Ezekiel, the spirit picks him up and transports him from the outer gates into the very center of the temple, and Ezekiel sees God's glory filling the inside of the temple. Yahweh makes a pronouncement for Ezekiel to hear and to pass on to others: "This is the place for my throne and the place for the soles of my feet, where I will dwell, in the midst of the people of Israel forever" (43:7). With these actions and words, Yahweh is once more ensconced in the temple, with a promise to remain there forever. Never again will God or people endure exile; at last, they are home. But now that they are home, there is still work to do. Yahweh's first words once back in God's own temple are very political in nature. God comments on the division of church and state in terms that we should remember even today.

The people of Israel will never again defile my holy name, neither the people themselves nor their kings through their unfaithfulness nor through the corpses caused by their kings on land's high places. The kings placed their entryways near my entryways and their doorways next to my doorways, with only a wall between me and them, and then they profaned my holy name through their abominations that they performed. So I consumed them in my anger. Now they should remove their unfaithfulness far away, and remove the corpses of the kings away from me, because I will dwell in their midst forever.

Ezekiel 43:7b–9

In ancient Jerusalem before Babylonia's conquest, the great temple for Yahweh stood right next to the massive palace for the kings. King Solomon, the son of David, had built both these structures with gargantuan amounts of slave labor. More accurately, the temple stood in the shadow of the much larger palace. Yahweh complains that these structures were so close that the actions of the kings affected the cleanliness of the temple. Political evil damaged the religious practices and the faith of the people. Certainly, there was a division between church and state in ancient Israel; in physical terms, it was the wall between the temple and the palace. But one of Ezekiel's key insights is that walls do not keep Yahweh in or out. The division between church and state is a very thin one, and Yahweh does not respect such boundaries.

Politics had destroyed the true religion of ancient Israel, according to this analysis. The kings' unfaithfulness, especially in the seeking of alliances with other nations, gnawed at the fibers of faith. Alliances themselves do not seem to be the problem; the true root of this predicament is the search for power and security. Those were the reasons that kings sought alliances; the friendship of a power such as Egypt would assure security and would provide more opportunities for the king to control Israel itself. The drive for power and security lures the kings away from God, and this diminished reliance upon God.

Politics and religion are closely intertwined; each has strong effects on the other. To deny this connection is not only folly; it can result in the inadvertent annihilation of the faith and of the people. According to Ezekiel, the requirements of faith must translate into political realities. In particular, the religion must resist and transform the politics of death, which only results in more corpses and a decreased faith. The politics of death takes many forms, from warfare to the impoverishment of others. Such deaths must be avoided, especially when it serves to increase the power and security of the elite few.

God's renewed presence in the temple is not the end of the story. God is not a prize to be possessed nor an automatic guarantee of blessings. Once God is in the temple again, God demands changes in the lives of the people. Yahweh will rule the people; no kings will be allowed to diminish the faith of the believers who are home from exile.

Purification (43:13–27)

The next step in the process of purification concentrates on the temple fixtures.[4] This process involves a week-long ceremony to dedicate the temple. Atonement requires that priests cleanse the altar from any sin that may have attached itself. For each of seven days, the priests offer a bull, a ram, and a goat upon the altar in specified ways. After these seven days of offerings, then the people can begin to use the temple and its altar for the more mundane sacrifices that people bring in response to their own needs.

The significance of this process of purification resides in its emphasis on worship. When the temple starts its service, the

---

[4] Cp. Leviticus 16. For a discussion of the issues involved in atonement of the temple, see Jon L. Berquist, *Ancient Wine, New Wineskins: The Lord's Supper in Old Testament Perspective* (St. Louis, Missouri: Chalice Press, 1991), chapter 9.

people might think of the benefits that they derive from it, such as the forgiveness and removal of sin. However, worship is the primary task of the temple; the other roles and functions derive from this. For the first week, the priests use the temple only for the praise of God and God's goodness. After the establishment of praise and worship within God's new house, then the other functions can begin, including the forgiveness of sin and the celebration of God's gifts of life.

Entering the Temple (44:1–14)

Ezekiel's guide takes him out of the temple itself, after delivering these instructions about the temple's first week of operation. Once outside, the prophet notices that the eastern gate, through which Yahweh had reentered, is now closed. Yahweh announces that the gate will remain shut forever. Yahweh will never leave again. There is, however, one person allowed to sit in that gate. The prince may take that place. In a sense, this is a place of great privilege, bestowing honor upon the prince who sits there.

But the eastern gate, in Ezekiel's vision, functions as a stark reminder. Once before, God left the temple, because of the sins of the kings. Now there will be no more kings, only a *nasî*. This is the same phrase that was applied to David in Ezekiel 34, and "prince" is not the best translation.[5] The term is best described as "chief" or "leader," referring certainly to an important person with political responsibilities, but not to the autocratic power of a king. The last king's sins resulted in the destruction of the people, and so God will never again allow a king. There will be, of course, political leaders, and the chief of those receives the privilege of sitting in the place that reminds the people of Yahweh's leaving. This leader cannot block Yahweh if God decides to leave again, but sitting in that place reminds everyone that the leader is responsible for making sure that politics never drive Yahweh from the temple again.

---

[5] See chapter 8.

The Levitical priests who had been so influential in religion under the monarchy also receive new assignments. Because of their inadequacy in their service in those earlier days, Yahweh reduces the Levites' roles. They will continually serve as a reminder of the problems of the former days, just as the prince sitting in the eastern gate will do. Yet Yahweh does not defrock these Levitical priests; there is still a place for them in the service of the temple. They continue to work right within the temple, because there is work for all of them. If these Levitical priests concern themselves with prestige, they will be quite disappointed, but if their first priority is service, their role in the temple will proceed.

Telling the Difference (44:15–31)

Another group of priests, the Zadokite priests, take over the main operations of the new temple.[6] The chief function of these priests is to tell the difference between the sacred and the holy. Difference is the most important concept for these priests. The priests' charge is to teach the people the difference between the holy and the unholy, the clean and the unclean (44:23). Again, cleanliness and holiness can become the chief concerns of the people. These are the truly vital issues for the priests and the ordering of the temple. Ezekiel and Yahweh desire the people to live holy lives. It is not just the presence of Yahweh that saves the people, nor the proper actions of the correct priests, but the holiness that diffuses throughout the entire people. In order to live holy lives, the priests must teach the people the difference, and the people must begin to recognize that their own actions make a difference. In the world that Yahweh creates in the restored Israel, then all the people must be holy. God's community requires active participation by all.

---

[6] Ezekiel's loyalty to the Zadokite group may reveal something of his lineage or his reliance on certain factions within the priesthood. The Zadokites may have been working toward dominance for generations, with success at last here in Ezekiel's time and writings.

In order for morality and worship to be the hallmarks of the community, all people must know their own responsibilities and must act upon them in moral ways, once they have learned the difference through the priests' teachings.[7]

Life Around the New Temple (45:1—48:35)

The presence of the new, active temple within the midst of the people affects their organization. Ezekiel explains how the tribes should divide the land. This repeats the themes of Israel's previous life. The old Exodus is now relived with the return of the people from exile, and temple construction follows immediately. The people receive law and instruction from God, through the priests. Monarchy is not replaced, but the establishment of the leader (*nasî*) takes over the place of the former kings. Still, one task remains: the division of the land among the tribes. In the old days, the tribes received land as they were able to conquer it, but Yahweh's new world leaves no room for military action. Thus, the priests divide the land for the people.

The temple is at the physical center of the whole nation. Jerusalem was too far south and east to be truly central, but now Israel's geography mutates to make the temple the literal center and focus of the people. From that center flows a river that waters the lands with life (47:1–12). This river sends out living water from the temple, enlivening the whole nation and all the people. Around the temple, each of the twelve tribes receives exactly equal portions. Everyone receives a fair share. God's fair share is the center, around which everyone else organizes his or her life.

This is another hallmark of the new community, just as worship and morality are key elements of what God builds among the restored people. There is fairness, and for Yahweh in this vision, fairness means equal distribution of resources. In the old world, each tribe could own whatever it could take;

---

[7] Distinguishing differences compares closely to the separation issues of holiness. See chapter 9.

but in God's new world, there is no rat race, no grasping of power and possessions. Everyone receives the same amount. Just as Yahweh reworks the religion and the politics and the morality of the renewed people, God transforms the economics in an extremely radical way. There is no more capitalist or monarchic distribution, in which inequality is expected, accepted, and affirmed. In God's brave new world, each receives an equal share because each person is equally God's child. Everyone deserves the richness of life, and everyone receives it.

The subject of the final chapter is Ezekiel's visions of a new temple in his chapters 40—48. This new temple is idealistic, but embodies in concrete form Ezekiel's values. In his vision, the temple resides in the very middle of the land, and all life proceeds from this new center. The twelve tribes arrange themselves in rectangular precision around the sacred spaces of the sanctuary. Symmetry gives birth to harmony, as all people live as one in Ezekiel's idealistic land. The worship of God is restored to its old glory, and more. Without kings or other politicians, the priests and a few leaders are the only government the people need, because they follow God in all things. Though Ezekiel's plan is thoroughly impractical and never came to pass, it is a beautiful statement of God's intentions. The people live in peace without needs to subjugate each other because God lives in their midst and because all people are willing to place God at their center.

This provides for a final statement of Ezekiel's chief message. When God is central among the people, then the world is in harmony. God expects the people to work with God in the salvation of the world. For a people who sit on the banks of the Great River in southern Babylonia, these are grandiose and thoroughly surprising visions. Though these people are victims, Ezekiel demands that they set as their goal the salvation of the world, the very world that has victimized them. God has not forgotten the exiles; instead, God moves to them to meet them at the point of their need. But God does not come just to give the people what they want; God comes to give the people a new mission, and that mission is expressed in surprisingly global terms.

God meets the people in Babylonia, going far out of the way to track them in the distant lands where their sin had taken them, then expects them to build a whole new society centered on God. So it is also with us. God meets us where we are, and then brings us back home to God and expects us to orient our own lives around God. Certainly this is not too much to ask after God has restored our lives to a deeply satisfying sufficiency that we never had before. When we become God's people in this way, then our name can be "Yahweh is there," just like the city of Ezekiel's vision (48:35).